THE DRAGON

The Dragon

A Satiric Fable in Three Acts

by

EUGENE SCHWARZ

Translated by
Elizabeth Reynolds Hapgood

HEINEMANN EDUCATIONAL
BOOKS LTD · LONDON

Heinemann Educational Books Ltd
LONDON EDINBURGH MELBOURNE
TORONTO AUCKLAND JOHANNESBURG
SINGAPORE IBADAN
HONG KONG
NAIROBI

SBN 435 23790 X

Heinemann Educational Books Ltd
(Drama Department)
The Press at
Kingswood
Tadworth, Surrey

Published by
Heinemann Educational Books Ltd
48 Charles Street, London W.1X 8AH
Printed in Great Britain by
Cox & Wyman Ltd,
London, Fakenham, and Reading

CONTENTS

CONTENTS

INTRODUCTION

EUGENE SCHWARZ was born in 1896. His father and mother had both been medical students, but the former's career was early interrupted by his arrest for revolutionary activities. Forbidden subsequent residence in St Petersburg, Moscow or any provincial capital, the family wandered from Ekaterinodar to Maikop, Ryazan, and other obscure towns whose names are unfamiliar to us.

Eugene seems, however, to have been allowed to enter Moscow University as a law student in 1913; but it was the stage, not the bar, that attracted him. All his mother's family had been amateur actors, his mother herself being one of the most talented.

'I remember a rehearsal,' Schwarz once said, recounting his earliest memory of the world of theatrical make-believe. 'I remember standing on the stage beside my mother and it seemed to me that I was lost among all the long dark skirts. So the very word for rehearsal for a long time revived that feeling whenever I heard it: the stage dimly lighted . . . a man with a beard explaining something . . . and I standing among the dark skirts, as in a forest, clutching my mother's hand.'

Soon abandoning law, Schwarz began to act himself, first in Rostov, then in Leningrad. But by 1923 he had discovered that his principal talent lay in writing, and by the time he was thirty-five a number of his stories, novels, film scripts, plays and fairy tales had been published. He wrote profusely: one play after another for the puppet theatre, film scripts, fairy tales, scripts for the circus or for platform readings.

One of his earliest dramatic works (1930) bore the title *Underwood*, named after the American typewriter that figures in the plot. Ostensibly a play about modern Soviet life, it was really a cross between a fairy tale and a detective story. In 1934 came *The Campaign of the Hohenstaufens* – modern satire again compounded with elements of fantasy.

Schwarz died in 1958. In 1960 a collection of his plays was published in an edition of four thousand copies (a small number of Russian standards). These were sold out by noon of publication day and the volume has not been reprinted. It included *The Dragon, The Naked King, The Shadow*, and other later plays: *The Deposit; The Snow Queen* (an adaptation of Hans Christian Andersen's famous fairy tale that is a popular component of Russian children's theatre repertoires); *Two Maples; An Ordinary Miracle;* and *A Story About A Young Couple.*

The Dragon was written in 1942. A highly controversial satire, it was rehearsed by Nikolai Akimov at his theatre in Leningrad and was given its first performance there the following year, only to be banned after three or four performances. It was then forgotten for almost two decades until its inclusion in the 1960 edition of his collected plays.

Schwarz was not specifically anti-Communist. He hated the Nazis, the Fascists, and anything that threatened personal liberty. That the Soviet authorities banned his work for two decades during the Stalin régime is rather more a self-indictment of them than an indictment of Eugene Schwarz.

In choosing the fairy story as his medium Schwarz followed a solid Russian literary tradition that goes back to Pushkin and beyond. The combination of satire with fantasy is also traditional. It was in connection with the fairy tale that Maxim Gorki once remarked upon 'the capacity of Russian thought to look far in advance of the fact'. It is in the nature of these folk stories that they 'fearlessly go out beyond the limits of reality'. In accepting the world of flying carpets and talking animals, three-headed dragons and helmets of invisibility, the spectator is asked to accept all the surrounding circumstances, too. And that is why the fairy-story-teller can travel so far into forbidden territory and come out unscathed. Whatever he says must be accepted as true equally when it defies the laws of gravity and the prevailing laws of the land.

Specialists apart, Eugene Schwarz's name has been practically unknown in the West, except as author of the scenarios for the two Soviet film masterpieces, *Cinderella* and *Don Quixote*. His adaptation for the children's theatre of *The Snow Queen* by Andersen was used as the basis for a version by Suria Magito and Rudolf Weil, produced at the Young Vic Theatre in London by Michel Saint-Denis (published by Heinemann Educational Books).

NORRIS HOUGHTON

CHARACTERS

SIR DRAGON

LANCELOT

CHARLEMAGNE, *Keeper of the Records*

ELSA, *his daughter*

BURGOMASTER

HENRY, *his son, also Footman-Secretary to Sir Dragon*

MR CAT

MR DONKEY

FIRST WEAVER

SECOND WEAVER

MASTER HATMAKER

MASTER OF MUSICAL INSTRUMENTS

BLACKSMITH

FIRST GIRL FRIEND OF ELSA

SECOND GIRL FRIEND OF ELSA

THIRD GIRL FRIEND OF ELSA

SENTRY

GARDENER

FIRST CITIZEN

SECOND CITIZEN

FIRST WOMAN CITIZEN

SECOND WOMAN CITIZEN

BOY

PEDDLER

JAILER

FOOTMEN, GUARDS, CITIZENS, CLERKS

ACT ONE

The scene is set in a spacious but cosy kitchen. It is very clean. There is a large hearth in the rear. The floor is made of stone and has a brilliant polish on it.
A CAT *is dozing in an armchair in front of the hearth. Enter* LANCELOT.

LANCELOT (*as he walks in he looks around and then begins to call*): Master Innkeeper! Mistress Innkeeper! Is there anyone here? Not a soul. . . . The house is empty, the gates are open, the doors are ajar, the windows unlatched. It's a good thing I am an honest man or I would be in a dither right now looking around for the most valuable thing to grab and then make my getaway as fast as I could. Whereas actually what I really want is to get a little rest.

He sits down.

I'll wait. Ah, Mr Cat! Are your masters coming back soon?

What? You won't speak?

MR CAT: No, I won't speak.

LANCELOT: Why not? Will you tell me that?

MR CAT: When you're in a soft, warm spot it's wiser to doze and keep your mouth shut.

LANCELOT: Yes, of course, but where are your masters?

MR CAT: They went out, and that suits me perfectly.

LANCELOT: Don't you love them?

MR CAT: I love them with every hair on my body, with my paws, with my whiskers, but they are threatened with a great sorrow. The only time I have any peace of mind is when they leave the premises.

LANCELOT: So that's how it is. But what threatens them? What kind of a threat is it? You're not going to tell me.

MR CAT: That's right, I'm not going to tell you.

LANCELOT: Why?

MR CAT: When you're in a soft, warm spot, it's better to doze and keep your mouth shut, rather than worry about any unpleasant future. Mee-ow.

LANCELOT: Now you've got me worried. It's so cosy here in the kitchen. I simply can't believe that this nice place, this handsome house, is threatened by any catastrophe. Mr Cat! What has happened here? Answer me! Come on!

MR CAT: Don't disturb the peace, Stranger.

LANCELOT: Listen, Mr Cat, you do not know who I am. I am a weightless man, as light as thistledown and am carried all over the world. I love to interfere in other people's affairs. As a result I have been slightly wounded nineteen times, seriously wounded five times and thrice I was mortally wounded. But I am still alive, and that is because I am not only as light as thistledown but also as stubborn as a mule. So now tell me, Mr Cat, what has happened here? It might turn out all of a sudden that I could rescue your masters. That has been done. Well? Come on now! What's your name?

MR CAT: Minnie.

LANCELOT: I thought you were – a tom.

MR CAT: Yes, I am, but people are so unobserving. . . . My masters still wonder why I don't have kittens. They say: What is the matter with you, Minnie? But they're sweet, the poor, uninformed creatures! Now I shan't say another word.

LANCELOT: But please, just tell me who your masters are?

MR CAT: He is Charlemagne, the Keeper of the Records, and she is his only daughter Elsa who has the gentlest little paws and is so sweet and quiet.

LANCELOT: Is she threatened?

MR CAT: Alas, she is, and so we all are.

LANCELOT: What is she threatened by? Go on . . .

MR CAT: Mee-ow! You see it is now four hundred years since dragon settled in our city.

LANCELOT: A dragon? That's fine!

MR CAT: He exacts a tribute from us. Every year he chooses a young girl. And we, without a single mee-ow, hand her over to the Dragon. He carries her off to his cave and we never see her again. They say they all die of loathing. F-fpfpt! Skat! F-f-f-t!

LANCELOT: Who are you speaking to?

MR CAT: The Dragon. Because he has chosen our Elsa! The damned lizard! F-f-f-t!

LANCELOT: How many heads does he have?

MR CAT: Three.

LANCELOT: That's a troika. And paws?

MR CAT: Four.

LANCELOT: I expected that. What about claws?

MR CAT: He has five on each paw.

LANCELOT: Nothing unusual there. Are they sharp?

MR CAT: As knives.

LANCELOT: And does he breathe fire?

MR CAT: He certainly does.

LANCELOT: You mean real flames?

MR CAT: They burn down forests.

LANCELOT: I see. Is he covered with scales?

MR CAT: He is.

LANCELOT: Thick ones?

MR CAT: Absolutely.

LANCELOT: How thick?

MR CAT: You can't scratch 'em with a diamond. Not that I ever tried.

LANCELOT: How big is he?

MR CAT: As big as a church.

LANCELOT: Well, I see it all now. Thank you, Mr Cat.

MR CAT: Will you fight him?

LANCELOT: I might.

MR CAT: I implore you to challenge him. He will, of course, do you in but before that happens, while we're lying here in front of the hearth we can dream about a miracle by which somehow or other, this way or that, perhaps, maybe, all of a sudden, it might just turn out that after all you killed him.

LANCELOT: Thank you, Mr Cat.

MR CAT: Pssst, pssst!

LANCELOT: What's happened?

MR CAT: They're coming.

LANCELOT: If only I find her attractive! If only I like her! That would be a great help. . . .

Ah! (*He looks out of the window.*)

I do like her! Mr Cat, she's a fine girl! But look, Mr Cat, what's that? She is smiling! She is completely calm! And her father has even a jolly look on his face. Have you been fooling me?

MR CAT: No, indeed. That's the saddest part of it all – they smile. Hush. I haven't said a word! . . .

Enter ELSA *and* CHARLEMAGNE.

LANCELOT: How do you do, Sir, and charming lady.

CHARLEMAGNE: How do you do, young man.

ELSA: Good day to you, Sir.

LANCELOT: Your home looked so inviting, the gates were open, a fire was burning in the kitchen, so I walked in without any invitation. Please excuse me.

CHARLEMAGNE: No need of that. Our doors are open to all.

ELSA: Do sit down. Give me your hat and I'll hang it behind the door. I'll lay the table right away . . .

LANCELOT *looks at her intently.*

What's the matter?

LANCELOT: Oh, nothing.

ELSA: I rather thought . . . well, you frightened me.

LANCELOT: No, no . . . I always look at people that way.

CHARLEMAGNE: Take a seat, my friend. I love strangers. I suppose it is because all my life I never stirred out of this town. Where do you come from?

LANCELOT: From far away.

CHARLEMAGNE: And did you have many adventures along the way?

LANCELOT: Alas yes, more than I liked.

ELSA: You must be tired. Do sit down.

LANCELOT: Thank you.

CHARLEMAGNE: You can have a good rest here. This is a very quiet town. Nothing ever happens here.

LANCELOT: Not ever?

CHARLEMAGNE: Never. Well, to be sure, last week we did have a high wind. The roof was nearly blown off one of the houses. But that's not really much of an event.

ELSA: Here's supper on the table. Please take your places. What's the trouble?

LANCELOT: You must excuse me but . . . you say this is a very quiet town?

ELSA: Of course.

LANCELOT: But . . . I have heard tales about . . .

   MR CAT *turns over.*

I have read something about a Dragon.

CHARLEMAGNE: Oh that . . . Well, we're so used to him. He's been living here for four hundred years.

LANCELOT: But . . . they told me . . . that your daughter . . .

ELSA: Sir Stranger . . .

LANCELOT: My name is Lancelot.

ELSA: Sir Lancelot then, forgive me and believe me I don't mean to give any orders but nevertheless I do ask you not to say a word about it.

LANCELOT: Why not?

ELSA: Because there is nothing to be done about it.

LANCELOT: Is that really so?

CHARLEMAGNE: Yes, there's nothing we can do. We have just been strolling around in the woods and we talked it all over in minute detail. Tomorrow, as soon as the Dragon takes her away, I will die.

ELSA: Papa, don't speak of it.

CHARLEMAGNE: That's all there is to say. That's all . . .

LANCELOT: Excuse me. There is one more question. Has no one ever tried to fight him?

CHARLEMAGNE: Not for the last two hundred years. Before that there were frequent attempts but he killed all of his attackers. He is an astounding strategist and a great tactician. He attacks his enemy suddenly, showering him with stones from above, then he hurls himself down right on to the head of his opponent's steed, sears him with flames and completely demoralizes his poor beast. Then he tears the rider to pieces with his claws. So you can understand why finally people ceased to oppose him. . . .

LANCELOT: Did the whole city ever attack him?

CHARLEMAGNE: It did.

LANCELOT: What happened?

CHARLEMAGNE: He burned up the suburbs and half the population went berserk from poisonous fumes. He's a great fighter.

ELSA: Do help yourself to the butter.

LANCELOT: Yes, yes, I'll have some. I must build up my strength. And so – please forgive me for pressing you with questions – no one is even attempting to challenge the Dragon any more? He has grown completely arrogant?

CHARLEMAGNE: Heavens, no! He's very kind.

LANCELOT: *Kind?*

CHARLEMAGNE: I assure you he is. When our city was threatened with an epidemic of cholera the municipal physician asked him to breathe fire on the lake. The whole town was saved from the cholera. Everybody had boiled water to drink.

B

LANCELOT: Was that long ago?

CHARLEMAGNE: Oh, not at all. It was only eighty-two years ago but a good deed like that is not forgotten.

LANCELOT: What other good deed has he ever done for you?

CHARLEMAGNE: Ah . . . let's see . . . well . . . he got rid of the gipsies for us.

LANCELOT: But gipsies – are such very nice people.

CHARLEMAGNE: What are you saying! How terrible! Of course, I have never seen a single gipsy. But I learned in school what dreadful people they are.

LANCELOT: How so?

CHARLEMAGNE: They are vagabonds by nature, it's in their blood. They are enemies of any organized government, otherwise they would have settled down and would not be wandering all over the place. Their sons lack virility, their ideas are destructive. They steal children.

ELSA: That's what they say.

CHARLEMAGNE: They infiltrate everywhere. Now we are completely rid of them, yet only a hundred years ago any dark-haired person had to prove that he did not have any gipsy blood.

ELSA: That's true.

LANCELOT: Who told you all this about the gipsies?

CHARLEMAGNE: Our dragon. The gipsies quite insolently opposed him from the very first years he was in power.

LANCELOT: Wonderful, intolerant people.

CHARLEMAGNE: You mustn't, you really must not talk like that.

LANCELOT: What does your dragon eat?

CHARLEMAGNE: Our city provides him with a thousand cows, two thousand sheep, five thousand chickens, and eighty pounds of salt a month. Summer and autumn there are in addition ten fields of lettuce, asparagus and cauliflower.

LANCELOT: He's eating you out of house and home!

CHARLEMAGNE: No, no, you are forbidden to say that! We are not complaining and, anyway, how else could we manage? As long as he is here – no other dragon would dare touch us.

LANCELOT: But all the other dragons were destroyed long ago.

CHARLEMAGNE: What if, suddenly, that turned out not to be the case? Really I assure you that the only way to get rid of dragons is to have your own. But that's enough about him, please. Now you tell us something interesting.

LANCELOT: All right. Do you know what The Book of Wrongs is?

ELSA: No, we don't.

LANCELOT: Then let me tell you. A five-years' walk from here in the Black Mountains, there is a huge cave. And in this cave lies a book, half filled with writing. No one ever touches it, yet page after page of writing is added day after day. Who writes in it? The world! The mountains, grass, stones, trees, rivers, they all see what people are doing. They know all the acts of criminals, all the woes of those who suffer unjustly From branch to branch, from drop to drop, from cloud to cloud all human wrongs are carried to the cave in the Black Mountains and set down in the Book, which grows and grows. If there were no such book in the world, the trees would wither from dejection, and the waters would turn bitter. And the people . . .

ELSA: What people?

LANCELOT: Me, for example. I am an observant fellow. I heard about this book and was not too lazy to go and look into it. Once you have read this book you never have another moment of peace. Oh, what a catalogue of wrongs it is! One cannot fail to respond to them.

ELSA: How is that?

LANCELOT: We involve ourselves in the affairs of others. We help those who must be helped. And we destroy those who must be destroyed. Do you want to be helped?

ELSA: How?

CHARLEMAGNE: In what way could you help us?

MR CAT: Mee-ow!

LANCELOT: I have been mortally wounded three times, and in each case by those whom I forcibly saved. Despite this, and although you do not ask it of me, I will challenge the Dragon! Do you hear what I say? Elsa?

ELSA: No no! He will kill you and that will poison the last hours of my life.

MR CAT: Mee-ow!

LANCELOT: I will challenge the Dragon to a battle!

An even louder whistling sound is heard, then noise, howling, roaring. The windows rattle. Red flashes are seen outside.

MR CAT: Speak of the devil. . . .

The howling and whistling suddenly stop. There is a loud knock on the door.

CHARLEMAGNE: Come in!

    HENRY enters, richly dressed as a footman.

HENRY: Sir Dragon to see you, Sir.

CHARLEMAGNE: Have him come right in!

    HENRY opens the doors wide. Pause. Enter, without haste, a solidly built, middle-aged but youthful-appearing, fair-haired man of military bearing. He has a broad smile on his face. His manner, except for a slight coarseness, is not without a suggestion of agreeableness. He is slightly hard of hearing.

DRAGON: Greetings, my children! Elsa my dear, how do you do! Ah, you have a guest, who is it?

CHARLEMAGNE: A traveller, passing through town.

DRAGON: What's that again? Speak up, distinctly, answer like a soldier!

CHARLEMAGNE: He's a traveller!

DRAGON: Not a gipsy?

CHARLEMAGNE: Of course not. He's a very nice man.

DRAGON: What's that?

CHARLEMAGNE: A very nice man.

DRAGON: All right, Mr Traveller! Why don't you look at me? Why are you peering out of the door?

LANCELOT: I am waiting for the Dragon to come in.

DRAGON: Ha, ha! I'm the Dragon!

LANCELOT: You? But I was told you have three heads, claws, and are huge!

DRAGON: Oh well, today I just dropped in informally, without my regalia.

CHARLEMAGNE: Sir Dragon has been living so long among human beings, that he occasionally turns himself into one and drops in to make a friendly call.

DRAGON: So I do indeed. We are real friends, my dear

Charlemagne. Indeed I am more than a friend to every
one of you. I am the friend of your childhood. More
than that I was the friend of your father's childhood,
your grandfather's, your great-grand-father's. I remember your great, great-grandfather in short
trousers.

He wipes his eye.

Dammit! An unwanted tear. . . . Ha, ha! Your guest's
eyes are popping out! You didn't expect such feelings
from me? Well, answer me! He's all embarrassed, the
idiot. Well, well, never mind. Ha, ha, Elsa!

ELSA: Yes, Uncle Dragon.

DRAGON: Give me your little paw.

ELSA *holds out her hand to the* DRAGON.

You darling little kitten! You rascal! What a warm
little paw! Hold your little chin up higher! Now
smile! That's it. What are you staring at, Stranger?
Eh?

LANCELOT: I am admiring you.

DRAGON: Good boy. You speak up distinctly. Go on
admiring. Everything is very straightforward with us,
Stranger. Hup, two, three. Soldier fashion. Eat!

LANCELOT: Thank you, I've had enough.

DRAGON: Never mind, eat! Why did you come here?

LANCELOT: On business.

DRAGON: What business? Well, come on – out with it!
Eh? Perhaps I can be of use to you. Why did you
come?

LANCELOT: To slay you.

DRAGON: Louder!

ELSA: No, no, he's just joking! Want to hold my hand
again, Uncle Dragon?

DRAGON: What for?

LANCELOT: I challenge you to combat, you, do you hear me?

The DRAGON is silent. His face is flushed.

I am challenging you a third time to combat, do you hear?

A frightful, ear-splitting triple roar is heard. Despite the volume of the roar, which makes the walls tremble, it is not altogether unmusical. There is nothing human in the roar. It is the roar of a dragon, who is balling his fists and stamping his feet.

DRAGON: *Suddenly stopping his roar, he speaks in a quiet tone.* Well, why are you silent? Are you frightened?

LANCELOT: No.

DRAGON: No?

LANCELOT: No.

DRAGON: Very well, then, watch this!

He makes a slight movement with his shoulders and suddenly an astounding change comes over him.

A new head appears on his shoulders and the earlier one disappears completely. A serious, self-controlled, narrow-faced, greying blond with a high forehead is standing in front of LANCELOT.

MR CAT: Do not be astonished, my dear Lancelot. He has three tops and he changes them around as he wishes. . . . What am I saying!

He hides in a corner.

DRAGON (*whose voice is as altered as his face, speaks rather softly but dryly*): Your name is Lancelot?

LANCELOT: It is.

DRAGON: Are you a descendant of the famous knight errant called Lancelot?

LANCELOT: He is a distant connection of mine.

DRAGON: I accept your challenge. Knights errant – they're the same as gipsies. You must be destroyed.

LANCELOT: I shall not surrender.

DRAGON: I have already destroyed eight hundred and nine knights, nine hundred and five people of unrecorded professions, one old drunkard, two lunatics, two women – the mother and aunt respectively of girls I had picked out – one twelve-year-old boy – the brother of another such girl. Besides, I have destroyed six armies and five mutinous mobs. Do sit down.

LANCELOT (*sitting down*): Thanks.

DRAGON: Smoke? Go ahead, don't mind me.

LANCELOT: Thanks.

He takes out a pipe and fills it in a leisurely fashion.

DRAGON: Do you know on what day I made my appearance in the world?

LANCELOT: An unhappy one.

DRAGON: On the day of a great battle. On that day Attila himself suffered a defeat. Can you imagine how many warriors lives it cost to accomplish that feat? The ground was soaked with blood. By midnight the leaves on the trees turned brown. By dawn huge black mushrooms – they called them cadaver mushrooms – had sprung up under the trees. And after them I crawled up out of the earth. The blood of dead Huns course through my veins – and it is cold blood. In combat I am cold, calm and exact in my aim.

As he says these last words he makes a slight movement with one hand. There is a dry clicking sound. From his

index finger a stream of flame comes out. It lights the pipe
which LANCELOT *has been filling.*

LANCELOT: Thanks.

He puffs his pipe with satisfaction.

DRAGON: You oppose me, therefore you oppose war?

LANCELOT: Goodness no! I have been fighting all my life.

DRAGON: You are a stranger here where the people and I have learned to understand one another. The entire city will look on you with horror and will be delighted to have you dead. You will meet an inglorious end. Do you realize that?

LANCELOT: No.

DRAGON: You are as determined as ever?

LANCELOT: Even more so.

DRAGON: You are a worthy opponent.

LANCELOT: Thanks.

DRAGON: I shall fight seriously.

LANCELOT: That suits me.

DRAGON: That means that I shall kill you promptly. Now. Here.

LANCELOT: But I am unarmed!

DRAGON: Do you expect me to give you time to arm yourself? No indeed. I told you I would put up a serious fight. I shall attack suddenly, right now . . . Elsa, bring a broom!

ELSA: What for?

DRAGON: I shall immediately reduce this fellow to ashes, and you are to sweep him up.

LANCELOT: Are you afraid of me?

DRAGON: I don't even know what fear is.

LANCELOT: Then why are you in such a hurry? Give me

until tomorrow. I'll get hold of some arms and we can meet out in a field.

DRAGON: Why that?

LANCELOT: So the people will see you are no coward.

DRAGON: The people won't know anything about it. These two will keep their mouths shut. You will die here and now, quietly, ingloriously.

He raises his arm.

CHARLEMAGNE: Stop!

DRAGON: What's the matter?

CHARLEMAGNE: You can't kill him.

DRAGON: What?

CHARLEMAGNE: I beg you. Don't get mad. I am completely devoted to you. But you see, I happen to be the Keeper of the Records.

DRAGON: What has your office to do with the present matter?

CHARLEMAGNE: I have a document in my safe-keeping which you signed three hundred and eighty-two years ago. This document has never been superseded. You understand, I am not making any objections, I am merely reminding you. It bears your signature – 'The Dragon'.

DRAGON: What of it?

CHARLEMAGNE: After all, this case does involve my daughter. And I really should like to see her live a little longer. That's perfectly natural, you know.

DRAGON: Be quick about it.

CHARLEMAGNE: You cannot kill him now. Anyone who challenges you is safe up to the day of battle – this is written and confirmed by you under oath. And the day of battle is fixed not by you but by the challenger. That's what the document says and it was sworn to. And the entire city is obligated to give aid to whoever challenges you, and no one is to be punished for this – that also is sworn to.

DRAGON: When was this document drawn up?

CHARLEMAGNE: Three hundred and eighty-two years ago.

DRAGON: I was very naïve in those days, a sentimental, inexperienced boy.

CHARLEMAGNE: But the document has never been superseded.

DRAGON: That makes no difference . . .

CHARLEMAGNE: But the document . . .

DRAGON: That's enough about documents. We're grown-up people.

CHARLEMAGNE: But you yourself signed it. . . .

ELSA: I can run and fetch it.

DRAGON: Don't you stir.

CHARLEMAGNE: We have found a man who is willing to try to save my little girl. Love for one's child – well, that doesn't count for much. We know about that. But there's also a question of laws of hospitality and that too is permissible. Why do you look at me so fiercely?

He covers his face with his hands.

ELSA: Papa! Papa!

CHARLEMAGNE: I protest!

DRAGON: All right. Now I'll wipe out this whole nest.

MR CAT: And all the world will learn that you are a coward!

DRAGON: How so?

MR CAT *jumps out of the window and hisses from out-side.*

MR CAT: I'll tell everything to everybody, everything to everybody, you old lizard.

The DRAGON *again lets out a roar. This time it is just as powerful but it gives evidence of definite hoarseness, sobbing and spasmodic coughing. This is the roar of a huge, very aged and evil monster.*

DRAGON (*suddenly ceasing to roar*): Very well, then. We shall have our fight tomorrow as you requested.

He leaves abruptly. Immediately outside the door, there are sounds of whistling, high wind, great noise. The walls tremble, the lamp flickers, then the sound gradually lessens in the distance.

CHARLEMAGNE: He's flown away! What have I done! I am a damned old fool. Yet I could not have acted differently! Elsa, you're not angry with me, are you?

ELSA: No, of course not! I am proud of you!

CHARLEMAGNE: I suddenly feel very weak. You must excuse me. I'll go and lie down. No, no, you mustn't come with me. Stay here with our guest. Entertain him with your conversation – he's been so very nice to us. I must lie down.

He goes out.

There is a pause.

ELSA: Why did you start all this? I am not reproaching you but – everything was settled. It is not so terrible to die young. Everyone else will grow old.

LANCELOT: Think what you're saying! Even trees sigh when they are cut down.

ELSA: But I am not complaining.

LANCELOT: Aren't you even sorry for your father?

ELSA: But after all he is going to die just when he wishes to do so. In essence, that's happiness.

LANCELOT: Aren't you sorry to say goodbye to your friends?

ELSA: No, for if I hadn't been chosen one of them would have been taken.

LANCELOT: And what of your fiancé?

ELSA: How did you know that I had a fiancé?

LANCELOT: I sensed it. And aren't you sorry to be separated from him?

ELSA: But the Dragon, in order to console Henry, has appointed him his personal secretary.

LANCELOT: In that case it's not too hard to leave him. What about your city? Aren't you sorry to go away from it?

ELSA: But it's for the sake of my city that I am going to my death.

LANCELOT: And does it accept your sacrifice so casually?

ELSA: No, no! If I die on Sunday the whole town will be in mourning until Tuesday. For three whole days no one will touch any meat. For tea they will serve special little cakes, called 'Poor Elsas' in memory of me.

LANCELOT: Is that all?

ELSA: What else could they do?

LANCELOT: Kill the Dragon.

ELSA: But that's impossible.

LANCELOT: The Dragon has corrupted your soul, poisoned your blood and dimmed your vision. But we shall set everything to rights.

MR CAT *runs in.*

MR CAT: Eight of my lady cat friends and forty of my kittens have run around to all the houses and told about the coming fight. Mee-ow! The Burgomaster is hurrying this way.

LANCELOT: The Burgomaster? That's fine!

The BURGOMASTER *enters, running.*

BURGOMASTER: How do you do, Elsa. Where's the stranger?

LANCELOT: Here I am.

BURGOMASTER: First of all be kind enough to lower your voice, use as few gestures as possible, move softly and look me in the face.

LANCELOT: Why?

BURGOMASTER: Because I have all the nervous and psychic diseases there are in the world and on top of them I have three that are still unidentified. Do you think it's easy to serve as a burgomaster under a dragon?

LANCELOT: I am going to kill the Dragon and you will feel better.

BURGOMASTER: Better? Ha, ha! Better! Ha, ha! Better!

He becomes hysterical. He drinks some water, and becomes calmer.

The fact that you have dared to challenge the Dragon – is a calamity. Everything was running smoothly. The Dragon kept my assistant under his influence – but then he's a rare scoundrel, and so are all his gang, the merchants and millers. Now everything is all upset. The Dragon will be getting ready for the battle, he will neglect matters of civic administration which he had only just begun to grasp.

LANCELOT: Try to get this into your head, you miserable creature: I am going to save your city!

BURGOMASTER: The city? Ha, ha! *My* city! The city! Ha, ha!

He drinks water and calms down again.

My son is such a scoundrel that I would sacrifice two cities if only I could be sure he would be destroyed. It's better to have five dragons than a snake in the grass like my son. I beg of you, go away.

LANCELOT: I will not go away.

BURGOMASTER: It's your luck, I am going into a cataleptic fit.

He freezes with a bitter smile on his face.

LANCELOT: But I am going to save you all! Try to understand!

The BURGOMASTER *does not reply.*

Do you understand?

The BURGOMASTER *remains silent.* LANCELOT *throws a glass of water in his face.*

BURGOMASTER: No, I don't understand you. Whoever asked you to fight him?

LANCELOT: The whole city wants me to do it.

BURGOMASTER: Yes? Well, look out of the window. The best people in town have hurried over here to beg you to clear out.

LANCELOT: Where are they?

BURGOMASTER: There they are, sticking close to the walls. Come nearer, my friends.

LANCELOT: Why are they walking on tiptoe?

BURGOMASTER: So as not to upset my nerves. Now,

my friends, tell Lancelot what you want him to do. All right. One! Two! Three!

CHORUS OF VOICES: Leave town! Hurry, please! This very day!

LANCELOT walks away from the window.

BURGOMASTER: You see? If you are a humane and civilized person you will submit to the will of the people.

LANCELOT: Not for anything!

BURGOMASTER: It's just your luck. I'm about to have a slight attack of madness.

He strikes a pose with one hand pressed to his side and the other in an affected gesture.

I'm a tea kettle, boil me!

LANCELOT: I can see why all those people tiptoed when they came here.

BURGOMASTER: Well, why?

LANCELOT: So they wouldn't wake up the *real* people. I'll go out and speak to them right away.

He rushes out.

BURGOMASTER: Boil me! Besides, what can he do? The Dragon will give the order and we'll put him in prison. My dear Elsa, don't get all upset. Any second now, when the appointed time comes our dear Dragon will take you to his bosom. You can be quite calm.

ELSA: I am calm.

There is a knock on the door.

Come in!

HENRY enters, still dressed as a footman.

BURGOMASTER: Hello, my boy.

HENRY: Hello, Papa.

BURGOMASTER: Have you a message from him? Of course, there will be no fight! Did you bring an order to clap Lancelot into prison?

HENRY: Sir Dragon sent the following orders: One: Fix the fight for tomorrow; Two: provide Lancelot with arms; Three: try to use your wits to better purpose.

BURGOMASTER: It's just your luck – I am going right out of my senses! Oh, my mind! Ouch! Help! Go away!

HENRY: I have orders to talk privately with Elsa.

BURGOMASTER: Orders? Oh, yes, of course. I'm going, I'm going, going.

He hurries out.

HENRY: Hello, Elsa.

ELSA: Hello, Henry.

HENRY: Do you expect that Lancelot will save you?

ELSA: No. How do you feel about it, Henry?

HENRY: I don't expect him to either.

ELSA: What did the Dragon order you to tell me?

HENRY: He ordered me to tell you that you are to kill Lancelot if it becomes necessary.

ELSA (*horrified*): How?

HENRY: With a knife. Here it is. And it has a poisoned tip . . .

ELSA: But I don't want to!

HENRY: Well, Sir Dragon ordered me to warn you that if you don't obey he will kill all your friends.

ELSA: Very well then, tell him I'll try.

HENRY: Sir Dragon also ordered me to tell you that any hesitation on your part will be punished as disobedience.

C

ELSA: I hate you!

HENRY: And Sir Dragon also ordered me to say that he knows how to reward faithful servants.

ELSA: Lancelot will slay your Dragon!

HENRY: To that, Sir Dragon ordered me to say: We shall see!

CURTAIN

ACT TWO

The scene is set in the central plaza of the city. To the right is the Town Hall with a tower beside which a sentry is stationed. In the background centre, is a huge, gloomy, brown building without any windows, it has a gigantic iron portal that reaches from top to bottom of the structure. Over it is a sign in Gothic script: 'Human Beings Keep Out.' To the left is the broad wall of an old fortress.

In the centre is a well with an open-work railing. HENRY, *without his livery, in an apron, is polishing the brass fixtures on the great iron portal.*

HENRY (*humming*): We shall see, we shall see, growled the Dragon. We shall see, we shall see, roared the old Dra-Dra-Dragon. Old Man Dragon, he thundered! We shall see! The devil take me. And indeed we shall see, tra-la-la!

> *The* BURGOMASTER *hurries out of the Town Hall. He is wearing a straitjacket.*

BURGOMASTER: 'Morning, my boy. Did you send for me?

HENRY: 'Morning, Papa. I wanted to find out how things are going with you. Is the session of the Municipal Board of Self-Government finished?

BURGOMASTER: I should say not! It took us all night and we barely got through the confirmation of the agenda for the day.

HENRY: Got pretty tired, didn't you?

BURGOMASTER: What do you think? They had to give me three fresh straitjackets in the last half-hour.

He yawns.

I don't know if it is the humidity or what, only today my damned schizophrenia is acting up like anything. I rave and I rave. . . . I have hallucinations, *idées fixes* . . .

He yawns.

Got a cigarette?

HENRY: Yes.

BURGOMASTER: Untie me. We can have a smoke.

HENRY unties his father. They sit down side by side on the steps of the Palace. They light cigarettes.

HENRY: When will you decide the question of arms?

BURGOMASTER: What arms?

HENRY: For Lancelot.

BURGOMASTER: For what Lancelot?

HENRY: Have you gone out of your mind?

BURGOMASTER: Of course. You're a fine son. You have completely forgotten that your poor old father is desperately ill.

He yells.

Oh, people, people, love ye one another!

He speaks quietly.

You see how I rave?

HENRY: There, there, Papa. You'll get over it.

BURGOMASTER: I know myself that it will pass. Nevertheless it is unpleasant.

HENRY: You listen to me. There is important news. Old Man Dragon is nervous.

BURGOMASTER: That's not true!

HENRY: I assure you it's so. Our old boy has been flying around all night, no one knows where, without any regard for his wings. It was nearly dawn when he reached home. He smelled horribly of fish, which is what always happens when he is worried. See?

BURGOMASTER: Yes, yes.

HENRY: And I was able to ferret this much out: our good old lizard was flying all over last night to find out all the dirt about our fine Sir Lancelot.

BURGOMASTER: Well?

HENRY: I don't know in what depraved haunts, whether in the Himalayas or on Mount Ararat, in Scotland or the Caucasus, but the old boy dug up the fact that Lancelot is – a professional hero. I despise little people of that sort! But the Dragon, as a professional villain, appears to lend some significance to this fact. He raged, squeaked, whimpered. Then he wanted some beer. Having swilled down a whole keg of his favourite brand, and without leaving any orders behind, the Dragon once more straightened up his flippers and since then he has been hurtling through the skies like a crazy bird. Doesn't this upset you?

BURGOMASTER: Not a whit.

MR CAT *slinks in and hides behind the well.*

HENRY: Papa, tell me – you are older than me, more experienced. . . . Tell me what you think about the coming fight? Please, Papa, answer me. It isn't possible that Lancelot could . . . Just give me a straight answer without any official double-talk. Surely Lancelot could not conceivably win, could he? Answer me, Papa.

BURGOMASTER: Please, my boy, I'll give you a straight-forward answer with all my heart. You see, boy, I am truly devoted to our old Dragon! I can give you my word of honour on it. I've come to feel about him as if he were a member of the family, almost. I even, well I don't really know how to put it to you, I even would like to sacrifice my very own life for him. That's God's truth and may I be struck down on the spot if it isn't! No, no, no, dearie, he will win! He'll win by some miracle-tentacle, hook or crook, some wing-sling – oh, how I love him! Love him! And that's that. There's your answer.

HENRY: Don't you want to speak heart to heart, Papa, with your only son?

BURGOMASTER: No, my boy, I don't. I'm not that crazy yet. Of course, I am off my head but not to that degree. Did the Dragon put you up to cross-examine me?

HENRY: Why, Papa! How can you say such a thing!

BURGOMASTER: You're a fine lad. You conducted the whole conversation in a prime style. I am proud of you. And not, I swear, just because I am your papa. I am proud of you as an expert, an old hand. You remember now what I have said to you?

HENRY: Of course.

BURGOMASTER: And even those little words about the wing-sling and so on?

HENRY: I recall them all.

BURGOMASTER: Well then go and report!

HENRY: Very well, Papa.

BURGOMASTER: Oh my one and only, my darling little
spy . . . You are making a fine little career for yourself. Need any money?

HENRY: No, not for the present, thank you, Papa.

BURGOMASTER: Take some, don't be shy. I am flush
now. I had a slight attack of kleptomania only
yesterday. Take some . . .

HENRY: Thanks. I really don't need any. But now come
on, tell me the truth. . . .

BURGOMASTER: What are you up to, my boy? You
talk like a little child – truth, truth . . . You see, I'm
not just anyone in this town, I'm the Burgomaster. I
haven't told the truth even to myself for so many
years that I have forgotten what it's like, the truth. In
fact it makes me dizzy, it turns me upside down. Do
you know what the damned thing smells like? But
that's enough about it, son. Hail to the Dragon! Hail
to the Dragon! Hail to the Dragon!

The sentry on the tower strikes his halberd on the ground.
SENTRY, *yelling.*

Attention! Eyes on the sky! His Excellency is appearing over the Grey Mountains!

HENRY *and the* BURGOMASTER *jump up and
straighten themselves and throw their heads back to look at
the sky. A faraway rumble is heard which gradually fades
away.*

At ease! His Excellency has turned back and disappeared in a cloud of fire and smoke!

HENRY: He's keeping watch.

BURGOMASTER: Just so. And now you answer a little
question for me: Did the Dragon really not give you
any instructions, my boy? Well?

HENRY: No, he did not, Papa.

BURGOMASTER: And we are not going to kill him?

HENRY: Kill whom?

BURGOMASTER: Our rescuer.

HENRY: Oh, Papa, Papa.

BURGOMASTER: Tell me, my boy. Didn't he order a knife to be struck on the Q.T. into Lancelot?

MR CAT: Pf-tt!

BURGOMASTER: Don't be shy about it, tell me . . . It's nothing . . . An everyday matter . . . Well, my boy? Are you going to keep your mouth shut?

HENRY: Yes.

BURGOMASTER: All right then, shut up. I understand. You can't do anything about it – it's your job.

HENRY: May I remind you, Sir Burgomaster, that any minute now a solemn ceremony will begin in order to present the arms to Sir Hero. It is possible that old Uncle Dra-Dra will choose to grace the ceremony with his presence, and you haven't got anything ready.

BURGOMASTER, *yawning and stretching*.

All right, I'll go. It will only take a second to scrape together some kind of arms. He'll be satisfied. Come here and tie up my sleeves. . . . Look, there he comes! Lancelot is here!

Hysterically.

Glory be to you, glory and hosanna! St George the Victorious! Oh, forgive me, in my raving I mixed up the names. I suddenly fancied that you looked like him.

LANCELOT: That's very possible. He is a distant connection of mine.

BURGOMASTER: What did you do to make the night pass quickly?

LANCELOT: I wandered around.

BURGOMASTER: Did you make friends with anyone?

LANCELOT: Of course.

BURGOMASTER: With whom?

LANCELOT: Your terror-stricken citizenry set their dogs on me. But your dogs are very sensible. It was with them I made friends. They understood me because they love their masters and wish them well. We strolled around together until dawn.

BURGOMASTER: Did you pick up any fleas?

LANCELOT: No they were fine, well-kept dogs.

BURGOMASTER: Do you recall their names?

LANCELOT: They asked me not to mention them.

BURGOMASTER: I can't stand dogs.

LANCELOT: That's too bad.

BURGOMASTER: They're too simple.

LANCELOT: Do you think that it's so simple to love human beings? These dogs are well aware of what kind of people their masters are. They weep but they love them. They are the real beings. Did you send for me?

BURGOMASTER: Get behind me. A stork squawked and nipped a snake with its sharp beak. Get behind me, said the king, and looked around to see the queen. Behind me a lot of pretty girls were flying astride delicate reeds. In short, yes, I did send for you, Sir Lancelot.

LANCELOT: In what way may I serve you?

BURGOMASTER: In the big emporium they have received a fresh wheel of cheese. A maiden's best ornament is – modesty and a transparent dress. At sunset the wild ducks flew over the cradle. They are waiting for you at the session of the Municipal Board of Self-Government, Sir Lancelot.

LANCELOT: Why?

BURGOMASTER: Why do linden trees grow on the Avenue of the Dragon's Claws? Why fight when you'd rather dance? Why stand still when you hear hoof-beats? The members of the Self-Government Board must see you personally to find out exactly what kind of arms are most suitable for you, Sir Lancelot. Let's go and show ourselves to them!

They leave.

HENRY, *singing.*

We shall see, we shall see, growled the Dragon; we shall see, we shall see, roared the old Dragon. We shall see, devil take me – and indeed we shall see!

ELSA *enters.*

Elsa!

ELSA: Yes, it's me. You sent for me?

HENRY: I did. It's a pity that sentry's up there on the tower. If it weren't for that truly regrettable circumstance, I would put my arms around you and give you a kiss!

ELSA: And I would give you a slap!

HENRY: Oh, Elsa, Elsa! You always were a little too goody-goody. But it was becoming to you. There always was something behind your modesty. The Dragon can sense that in girls. He always picked the rascally little grasshoppers. Has Lancelot tried yet to make any advances?

ELSA: Shut up.

HENRY: Well, anyhow, I don't expect he has. Even if an

old hag were in your place, he'd go out and fight for her. He doesn't care whom he rescues. That's the way he was trained. He hasn't really ever taken a good look at you.

ELSA: But we've only just met.

HENRY: That's no excuse.

ELSA: Did you send for me just to tell me all this?

HENRY: Oh, no. I asked you to come so that I could say: Will you marry me?

ELSA: Do stop this nonsense.

HENRY: I'm not joking. I am authorized to tell you the following: if you are obedient and kill Lancelot in case of necessity, then as a reward the old Dragon will let you go free.

ELSA: No, no! I couldn't.

HENRY: Let's talk this out. Instead of you another girl will be chosen, someone you don't know at all, from the lower classes. She was actually listed for next year. So now you choose: which is better, to die a stupid death or live, full of joys such as you have only dreamed of, and at that only on rare occasions.

ELSA: He's turned coward!

HENRY: Who? The Dragon? I know all his weaknesses. He's willful, brutal, a leech – anything you want to name but not a coward.

ELSA: Yesterday he was threatening and today he is bargaining?

HENRY: It was I who persuaded him to that.

ELSA: You?

HENRY: I am the real conqueror of the Dragon, if you want to know: I can wheedle anything out of him. I waited for a chance – and I got it.

ELSA: I don't believe you.

HENRY: Yes, you do.

ELSA: Anyhow I can't kill a person!

HENRY: But I see you brought the knife along. It's dangling at your belt. I must be going now, darling. I have to put on my gold braid. But I am going away serene. You will carry out your orders for your own sake and for mine. Just think: Life, all of life is before us – if you wish it. Think it over.

    HENRY *leaves, and* MR CAT *comes nearer* ELSA.

ELSA: Good heavens! My cheeks are burning as if I had kissed him! What shame! He almost talked me into . . . Yes, Mr Cat, I must be that kind of a girl. . . . All right then . . . So be it. And it's all to the good. Enough! I have been the most obedient girl in town. I believed everything. And where did it get me?

Yes, everyone looked up to me but happiness was for the others. They are sitting at home at this moment, choosing their fanciest dresses, pressing their frills, curling their hair. Oh, I can just see them in front of their mirrors, primping and saying: 'Poor Elsa, poor girl, she was such a good girl!' They will all come to watch me all alone in the middle of the plaza, suffering. And that fool of a sentry will be staring at me and thinking about what the Dragon will do to me today. Tomorrow he'll still be alive and he will have his leave after his day on duty. He will stroll around. Then this stupid soldier will be telling everyone how some gay music was played, how people cried, when the Dragon carried me off to his lair. No, I refuse. I want to see everything, hear everything, feel everything. I want to be happy! This knife I brought to kill myself, but I shan't!

LANCELOT *runs out of the Town Hall.*

LANCELOT: Elsa! What a joy to see you!

ELSA: Why?

LANCELOT: Oh, my lovely young lady, I have such a hard day ahead of me that my soul craves a little peace, if only for a moment. And now, as if on purpose, I suddenly meet you.

ELSA: Were you at the session?

LANCELOT: I was.

ELSA: Why did they send for you?

LANCELOT: They offered me money if I would only abandon the fight.

ELSA: And what was your reply?

LANCELOT: I answered: You poor fools! . . . Let's not even talk about them. Elsa, you seem even lovelier today than yesterday. That is a sure sign that I like you. Do you believe that I will free you?

ELSA: No.

LANCELOT: Well, I am not offended. That, too, is a sure sign that I like you.

ELSA'S GIRL FRIENDS *enter.*

FIRST FRIEND: Here we are!

SECOND FRIEND: We – are Elsa's best friends.

THIRD FRIEND: We have lived side by side since we were babies.

FIRST FRIEND: She was always the cleverest of us all.

SECOND FRIEND: She was the nicest of us all.

THIRD FRIEND: And she loved us. She would mend our clothes, or she would solve our problems and comfort us when we felt we were the unhappiest creatures on earth.

FIRST FRIEND: We aren't late, are we?

SECOND FRIEND: You're really going to fight him?

THIRD FRIEND: Sir Lancelot, couldn't you get us places on the roof of the Town Hall? They wouldn't refuse a request from you. And we could see the fight so much better from there.

FIRST FRIEND: Oh, but you are angry.

SECOND FRIEND: And you don't want to talk to us.

THIRD FRIEND: But we're really not such a bad lot.

FIRST FRIEND: You think we came here on purpose to prevent you from saying goodbye to Elsa.

SECOND FRIEND: We didn't really come on purpose.

THIRD FRIEND: It was Henry who told us not to leave you alone with her until the Dragon permits. . . .

FIRST FRIEND: He told us to chatter.

ALL THREE FRIENDS: So we're chattering away like mad.

THIRD FRIEND: Because if we didn't we'd cry. And you, a stranger, have no idea what a disgrace it is here to cry or look unhappy in front of outsiders.

CHARLEMAGNE *comes out of the Town Hall.*

CHARLEMAGNE: The session is over, Sir Lancelot. The resolution on the arms for you was passed. You must forgive us, unfortunate murderers that we are, Sir Lancelot.

There is a flourish of trumpets. Serving men run out of the Town Hall, putting down carpets, and setting arm-chairs about. A particularly large and gorgeously orna-mented armchair is placed in the middle. To the right and to the left the chairs are much simpler. The BURGOMASTER

comes out of the Town Hall, surrounded by the members of
the Municipal Self-Government Board. He is in a jolly
mood. HENRY, *in his full dress uniform, attends them.*

BURGOMASTER: That was a good one . . . What was it
she said? 'I thought all boys knew how to do it.' Ha,
ha, ha! Do you know this one? Very funny. A certain
gipsy got his head cut off . . .

There is a blare of trumpets.

Ah, I see everything is ready . . . All right, I'll tell it to
you after the ceremony . . . Just remind me. Let us
begin, gentlemen, let us begin. We shall soon be
through.

The MEMBERS *of the Municipal Self-Government*
Board line up on either side of the great armchair. HENRY
stations himself behind it. The BURGOMASTER *bows*
to the chair. He begins to speak very rapidly.

We are moved and thrilled by the confidence which
Your Excellency has shown in us in allowing us to
carry out such important decisions. And we beg you
to take the chair as our honoured President. We ask it
once, we ask it twice, we –

He pauses.

ask it thrice. We are disappointed but we must begin
the proceedings without you. Gentlemen, be seated.
I declare the session . . .

There is a pause.

Water!

A manservant brings water from the well. The BURGO-
MASTER *drinks it.*

I declare the session to be . . . Water!

He drinks, clears his throat, then speaks in a very high
voice.

I declare. . . .

He continues in a deep bass voice.

the session . . . Water!

He drinks. Then in a high voice.

Thank you so much.

In his natural voice.

It's just your luck, gentlemen, I am going into a split personality.

In a bass voice.

What are you doing, you old ninny?

In a high voice.

Don't you see I am presiding at a meeting?

In a bass voice.

What makes you think it's a woman's job?

In a high voice.

Well, I don't like it either, darling. Don't leave me sitting on a point, let me make my point of order

In his natural voice.

You have heard the resolution to equip a certain Lancelot with weapons. We agreed to do it, but reluctantly. Hey, you there! Bring on the arms!

Trumpets blare. Men servants come in. The first one gives LANCELOT *a small brass bowl to which some thin straps are attached.*

LANCELOT: Why that's a barber's basin.

BURGOMASTER: Yes, but we designate it to be worn as a helmet. And that little brass tray can serve as a shield. Don't be uneasy! Even the objects in our city are obedient and disciplined. They will carry out their functions most conscientiously. We unfortunately have no knightly armour in the storehouse. But we do have a lance.

He hands LANCELOT *a slip of paper.*

This is a document to prove that the lance is actually out being repaired – the signature and attached seal verify the fact. You can hand it to the Dragon during the fight and the matter will all be properly adjudicated. There, now you have everything.

In a bass voice.

Close the session, you old ninny!

In a high voice.

But I am, I am closing it, drat it. What are the people so mad about, mad all the time and don't know why they're mad?

He sings.

Two, four, six, eight, out walked the handsome Knight . . .

In a bass voice.

Close the session, you blithering fool!

In a high voice.

What do you think I'm doing?

He sings.

Suddenly up the Dragon flew, and the handsome Knight he slew. . . . Bang, bang, oy-yo-yoy. I declare the session closed.

SENTRY: Attention! Eyes on the sky! His Excellency is appearing about the Grey Mountains and is flying this way at a terrific speed.

Everyone jumps up and stands frozen at attention looking up into the sky. There is a distant rumble which grows louder and louder with terrifying rapidity. It grows dark on the stage. A complete fog descends. The noise stops. Attention! His Excellency, like a storm cloud, is flying over you and has shut out the sun. Hold your breath!

There are two flashes of greenish light.

MR CAT (*whispering*): Lancelot, it's me the cat.

LANCELOT (*whispering back*): I recognized you straight away.

MR CAT: I am going over to doze on the fortress wall. Choose your time and come over to join me, and I'll purr something extremely agreeable in your ear.

SENTRY: Attention! His Excellency is dropping head first down into the Plaza.

There is an ear-splitting whistle and roar. Lights flicker. There is suddenly someone sitting curled up in the big armchair – a tiny, deathly pale old man.

MR CAT (*from the wall of the fortress*): Don't be alarmed, my dear Lancelot. This is his third head. He switches them as he pleases.

BURGOMASTER: Your Excellency! In the civic duties of municipal self-government entrusted to me there has been no incident. Except in the outskirts where one . . . to wit . . .

DRAGON (*speaking in a cracked, high treble voice*): Go away! Everyone get out! Except the stranger.

All go out, leaving on stage only the DRAGON, LANCELOT and MR CAT who is dozing on the fortress wall, rolled up into a ball.

How's your health?

LANCELOT: Thanks, perfect.

DRAGON: What's that tiny little basin on the ground?

LANCELOT: A weapon.

DRAGON: Did my people dream that up?

LANCELOT: They did.

DRAGON: The shameless creatures! I suppose you are offended?

LANCELOT: Not in the least.

DRAGON: That's a lie. My blood is cold but even I would be offended. Are you frightened?

LANCELOT: No.

DRAGON: Lies, lies! My people are very terrible. You won't find any others like them. That's my work. I made them what they are.

LANCELOT: Still they are human beings.

DRAGON: They only look like them.

LANCELOT: That's not so.

DRAGON: If you could see into their souls, oh, but you would tremble.

LANCELOT: I don't agree.

DRAGON: You would flee. You wouldn't sacrifice your life for a bunch of cripples. I myself, my dear fellow, personally crippled them. As it became necessary I crippled them. The human spirit, my dear fellow, is very lively. You can cut a man's body in two and he will die. If you tear his soul out, he becomes submissive. No, no, you won't find any souls anywhere like the ones here. These are souls without arms, souls without legs, deaf-mute souls, chained souls, hounded souls, branded souls. Do you know why the Burgomaster pretends to be crazy? To hide the fact that he has no soul at all. Then there are the souls full of holes, sold-out souls, burnt-out souls, dead souls. No, no, it's just too bad they are invisible.

LANCELOT: That's your good fortune.

DRAGON: How so?

LANCELOT: People would be frightened if they could see with their eyes what their souls have become. They would rather die and then you wouldn't have your slave people any more. Who would feed you?

DRAGON: God only knows. Perhaps you have something there. Well, shall we start?

LANCELOT: Very well, let's.

DRAGON: First say goodbye to the girl for whose sake you are going to your death. Hey there, boy!

   HENRY *enters, running.*

Bring Elsa!

   HENRY *runs out.*

You like the girl I chose?

LANCELOT: Very, very much.

DRAGON: I'm glad to hear it. I too like her very, very much. She's a fine girl. And an obedient one.

   Enter HENRY *with* ELSA.

Come here, come over here, my dear. Look me in the eye. That's right. That's a good girl. Your eyes are clear. You may kiss my hand. Fine! Your lips are warm. That shows your soul is at peace. Do you wish to say farewell to Lancelot? Go along. Speak sweetly to him.

   Then in a low voice.

Sweetly, sweetly. Kiss him goodbye. Don't be embarrassed. I'll be here. It's all right if I am here. And then kill him. That's all right, perfectly all right. After all I am here. You will do it in front of me. Go along. You can go over there with him, farther away. I have excellent eyesight. I'll see it all. Go along.

   ELSA *approaches* LANCELOT. MR CAT *is awake now and watching.*

ELSA: Sir Lancelot, I have been told to take farewell of you.

LANCELOT: Very well, Elsa. Let us say goodbye in any case. The fight will be a hard one. No one knows what the outcome will be. In bidding you adieu I want to tell you that I love you, Elsa.

ELSA: Me!

LANCELOT: Yes, Elsa. Already yesterday I liked you so very much, from the instant I looked out of the window and saw how quietly you walked home with your father. Now I realize that each time we meet you seem more and more beautiful. Oho, I said to myself. This is it. Then when you kissed the Dragon's paw, I was not angry with you, I was only very upset. Then I knew why: I love you, Elsa. Do not be angry, I did so much want you to know this.

ELSA: I thought you were going to challenge the Dragon anyhow. Even if there had been another girl in my place.

LANCELOT: Of course, I would have challenged him. I can't abide these dragons. But for your sake I would be ready to strangle him with my bare hands, although that would be unnecessary heroics, wouldn't it?

ELSA: You do love me?

LANCELOT: Very much. It rather scares me to think about it. If yesterday, when I came to the crossroads where there are three ways, I had turned either to the right or to the left we should never have met. That would have been terrible, wouldn't it?

ELSA: Yes, indeed.

LANCELOT: It's terrible to think about. There is no one in the world closer to me than you, even your town is my town because you live here. If I am . . . well, in short, if we never have another chance to talk together, you won't forget me.

ELSA: No.

LANCELOT: Don't forget me. There now you have looked straight at me for the first time today. And I feel warm all over, just as if you had caressed me. I am a wanderer, a high-hearted man whose whole life has been spent in fighting. A dragon here, cannibals there, giants . . . Work, work . . . And hard, ungrateful work at that. But I have always been happy. I never grew tired of it. And I often fell in love.

ELSA: Often?

LANCELOT: Of course. You travel around, you get into fights, you meet girls. They are for ever being captured by robbers, pushed into a bag and carried off to some giant, or being prepared to be boiled by cannibals. So it sometimes happens that you fall in love. But was it ever like this? I amused them. But as for you, Elsa, if we were only alone I'd kiss you again and again. Truly I would. And I would take you away. Together we would wander through the forests and over the mountains – it's not difficult at all. No, I'd get a steed for you with just the right kind of saddle so you would never get tired. And I would walk at your stirrup and gaze on you with admiration. And not anyone would ever dare to harm you.

ELSA *takes* LANCELOT's *hand. Music is heard.*

DRAGON: Good girl. She has him where she wants him.

HENRY: She's far from stupid, Your Excellency.

LANCELOT: Why, Elsa, are you going to cry?

ELSA: I am.

LANCELOT: Why?

ELSA: I'm so sorry . . .

LANCELOT: For whom?

ELSA: For myself, and you. We shall never see happiness together, Sir Lancelot. Why was I ever born into the world of the Dragon?

LANCELOT: I always speak the truth. We will be happy together. Believe me.

ELSA: Oh, don't . . . don't . . .

LANCELOT: We shall walk along the forest trail, happy and gay. Only you and I.

ELSA: No, no, you mustn't . . .

LANCELOT: And the sky above us will be clear. No one will drop down on us from there any more.

ELSA: Is that really true?

LANCELOT: That is the truth. Alas, does anyone in your city know how people can love one another? Terror, exhaustion, lack of confidence will be burned out of you for ever by my love. And when you fall asleep it will be with a smile on your face, and you will wake up smiling and call to me – that is how you will love me. You will come to love yourself too. You will walk with serenity and pride. You will realize that if this is the girl I kiss she must be good. The trees in the forests will speak to us caressingly, and the birds and the beasts – for true lovers can understand everything and they are in harmony with all the world. Everyone will welcome us because true lovers bring good fortune.

DRAGON: What little tune is he singing to her?

HENRY: He's preaching. Learning is light, ignorance is

darkness. Wash your hands before meals. And so forth and so on. The old stuff!

DRAGON: Aha. Now she has put her hand on his shoulder! Good for her.

ELSA: Even if we do not live to see such happiness, it makes no difference, for I am already happy now. Those monsters are watching us, yet we have gone far, far away. No one ever spoke to me as you have done. I did not know that the earth held people like you. Yesterday I was still cowed; I did not even dare to think about you. Yet during the night I stole downstairs and drank the wine you had left in your goblet. It is only now that I have realized that secretly, secretly, in my own way, I kissed you in the night because you had come to my defence. You cannot imagine how mixed up the feelings are in us poor, oppressed girls. Oh, my darling! I love you – and what happiness it is to say that right out to you . . . What a joy.

Kisses LANCELOT.

DRAGON, *stamping his feet impatiently*.

Now she'll do it, now she'll do it, now she'll do it!

ELSA: And now, dearest, let me go.

She extricates herself from LANCELOT's *embrace and draws the knife from her belt.*

Do you see this knife? The Dragon ordered me to kill you with this knife. Look!

DRAGON: Well! Well! Well!

HENRY: Go to it! Go to it!

ELSA *flings the knife into the well.*

The despicable creature!

DRAGON (*growling*): How dare you!

ELSA: Not another word from you! Do you think I would let you heap abuse on me now that he has kissed me! I love him. And he will slay you.

LANCELOT: That's the truth, Sir Dragon.

DRAGON: Well, well, well! We shall have to fight.

He yawns.

Yes, to be quite frank I don't really regret it because I just recently worked out a rather odd blow with one of my paws in an 'N' to 'X' manœuvre. Now I can try it out. Henry, call the guard.

HENRY *runs out. To* ELSA.

Go home, you little ninny and after the fight we'll have a little heart to heart chat.

HENRY *comes back with the guard.*

Listen, sergeant, there was something I wanted to say to you. . . . Oh, yes . . . Conduct this young lady to her home and guard her there.

LANCELOT *takes a step forward.*

ELSA: No, don't. You must save up your strength. When you have killed him come for me. I shall be waiting and meanwhile I shall be thinking of every word you said to me today. I believe in you.

LANCELOT: I will come for you.

DRAGON: Well, that's settled. Go along now.

The guard accompanies ELSA. *They leave.*

Henry, get that sentry down off the tower and put him in prison. He will have to have his head chopped off tonight. He heard that female talking back to me and he might gossip about it in his barracks. Make the arrangements. Then come back and smear my claws with poison.

HENRY *runs out. To* LANCELOT.

And you stay here, understand? And wait. I shan't
say when I'll begin. Hot warfare begins suddenly.
See?

*He climbs down out of his chair and goes off into the
palace.* LANCELOT *walks over to* MR CAT.

LANCELOT: Well, Mr Cat, what was that pleasant news
you were going to purr into my ear?

MR CAT: Look over there on the right, my dear Lancelot. In that cloud of dust there is a little donkey. He is
balking. Five people are trying to reason him out of
his stubbornness. Now I'm going to sing them a little
song.

He caterwauls.

Look, that stubborn beast is rushing right this way.
But near the wall he will balk again, then you talk to
his drivers. Here they are.

*Over the wall one sees the head of a donkey who stops
short in a cloud of dust. Five men yell at him.* HENRY
rushes across the square.

HENRY (*to the men*): What are you doing here?

TWO WEAVERS (*simultaneously*): We are bringing
merchandise to town, your honour.

HENRY: What kind of merchandise?

TWO WEAVERS: Carpets, your honour.

HENRY: Move on! Move on! It is forbidden to halt near
the palace.

DRAGON (*from within the palace*): Henry!

HENRY: Move along, move along.

He runs quickly into the palace.

TWO WEAVERS (*in unison*): Good day to you, Sir
Lancelot. We – are your friends, Sir Lancelot.

They clear their throats in unison.

H'm, h'm. Don't be annoyed if we speak at the same time – we've worked together since we were children and we have operated together so closely that we think and speak as one. We even fell in love on the same day, instantly, and we married twin sisters. We have woven many carpets but the best one we made for you.

They take a rug from the back of the donkey and spread it out on the ground.

LANCELOT: What a beautiful carpet!

TWO WEAVERS: Yes. It is of the very best quality, it is made of double threads, one of wool and one of silk, and the colours were prepared in accordance with our special secret formula. But the secret of the carpet does not lie in the wool, or the silk, or the colours.

In a low voice.

– it is a *flying carpet!*

LANCELOT: Splendid! Tell me quickly how to make it work.

TWO WEAVERS: It is very simple, Sir Lancelot. This corner is for rising – there is a sun woven here. This corner is for coming down – the earth is woven on it. This corner is for stunt flying – it has swallows on it. And this – is the dragon corner. You turn it up and you will drop vertically, right on your enemy's head. The design woven here is of a beaker of wine and fine food. Conquer and feast! No, no, don't thank us. Our great-grandfathers were out watching on the road, waiting for you to come. Our grandfathers waited too. And now we, their sons, have not waited in vain.

They go away quickly, and immediately the HAT-
MAKER *comes up hastily to* LANCELOT *with a cardboard
box in his hands.*

HATMAKER: How do you do, sir. Excuse me, but
kindly turn your head like this. And now like that.
Fine! I, sir, am a hatmaker, a master hatmaker. I make
the best hats and caps in all the world. I am very
famous in this town. Every dog knows me.

MR CAT: And every cat too.

HATMAKER: You see! Without taking any measure-
ment of a client, just by my eye, I make things which
are astonishingly becoming, and that is my joy in life.
There is one lady, for instance, whom her husband
loves only when she is wearing a hat fashioned by
me. She even sleeps in it and she goes around telling
everyone that she owes her life's happiness to me.
All last night I worked for you, sir, and I cried like
a child.

LANCELOT: Why was that?

HATMAKER: It's because of the sad, special style of the
cap I was working on: it is a *cap of invisibility*.

LANCELOT: Marvellous!

HATMAKER: As soon as you put it on you will disappear, and I will never know whether it is becoming
to you or not. Take it, but do not try it on while I am
here. I couldn't bear it! No, I couldn't bear it!

He runs out. LANCELOT *is immediately approached by
the* BLACKSMITH, *a bearded, saturnine fellow with a roll
on his shoulder. He undoes the parcel and produces a sword
and lance.*

BLACKSMITH: There! I worked at my forge all night.
Good luck to you.

Goes away. The MASTER OF MUSICAL INSTRU-
MENTS *hurries over to* LANCELOT. *He is a grey-haired
little man with a stringed instrument in his hands.*

MASTER OF MUSICAL INSTRUMENTS: I am the
Master Musical Instrument Maker, Sir Lancelot. My
great, great, great-grandfather began building this
little instrument. From generation to generation we
have worked on it and in human hands it has itself
become a human being. It will be your faithful com-
panion during your battle. Your hands will be busy
with sword and lance but it will take care of itself. It
will act as its own tuning fork and tune itself. It will
replace any string that breaks, it will play itself. When
needed it will play an encore, or when it is appropriate
it will remain silent. Isn't that so?

The instrument replies with a musical phrase.

You see? . . . We heard, we all heard how you
wandered, lonely, through our town and we hurried,
hurried to supply your needs from head to foot. We
have been waiting, hundreds of years we and our
ancestors have been waiting. The Dragon made us so
very quiet, so we have been waiting, oh, so quietly.
And now our waiting is over. Slay him and let us out
to freedom. Am I right?

The instrument responds with a musical phrase. The
MASTER OF MUSICAL INSTRUMENTS *goes out
bowing.*

MR CAT: When the battle will begin we, the donkey and
I, will take shelter in the barn behind the palace so
that the flames will not singe my fur. If you need anything, just call us. Here in the cooler on the donkey's
back is a refreshing drink, some cherry tarts, a

sharpener for your sword, spare points for your lance, needles and thread.

LANCELOT: Thank you.

He steps on to the carpet, picks up his weapons, slings the musical instrument over his shoulder. He takes hold of the Cap of Invisibility, puts it on, and disappears.

MR CAT: Perfect workmanship. Those men did an excellent job. Are you still here, my dear Lancelot?

LANCELOT (*from above*): No. I am rising slowly. Au revoir, my friends. Wish me luck!

MR CAT: Goodbye, my dear Lancelot. Ah, what worries, what cares! No, I must say that to be in bondage is much easier. You doze and don't expect anything. Am I right, Donkey?

The DONKEY wiggles his ears.

I don't know the ear language. Let's talk in words. We are not well acquainted with each other, but since we are working together, we can have a friendly chat. It really would be torture to have to wait around and not have anything to speak to.

DONKEY: But I refuse to mee-ow.

MR CAT: Well then let's talk like humans. The Dragon thinks Lancelot is still here but by now the scent is cold. Fun, isn't it?

DONKEY (*gloomily*): What fun?

MR CAT: Why don't you laugh?

DONKEY: I'd be beaten. As soon as I begin to laugh out loud, people say: that damned Donkey is howling again. And I get beaten.

MR CAT: So that's it! You mean you have such a penetrating laugh?

DONKEY: Yes.

MR CAT: What do you laugh at?

DONKEY: It all depends . . . I think and think until I remember something funny. Horses make me laugh.

MR CAT: Why?

DONKEY: They're such . . . asses.

The DONKEY *brays*.

MR CAT: Be careful. We'll be discovered. . . . Forgive me if I am indiscreet, but I've been wanting to ask you something for a long time. . . .

DONKEY: Well?

MR CAT: How can you eat thistles?

DONKEY: Why not?

MR CAT: In munching grass you do, of course, come across succulent little stems. But thistles! Really! They're so . . . sharp!

DONKEY: That doesn't bother me. I like highly seasoned food.

MR CAT: What about meat?

DONKEY: What's that?

MR CAT: Did you never try it?

DONKEY: I'm a vegetarian.

MR CAT: What about milk?

DONKEY: That I did drink when I was young.

MR CAT: Well, thank goodness, we shall be able to chat about some pleasant and comforting things.

DONKEY: Quite right. There are pleasant and comforting memories associated with it. Mother was kind. The milk was warm. That was heaven! So good.

MR CAT: Milk is good to lap up too.

DONKEY: I wouldn't do that.

MR CAT (*jumping up*): Did you hear that?

DONKEY: The beast is stamping his feet.

There is a howl from all three throats of the DRAGON *offstage.*

DRAGON (*offstage*): Lancelot!

There is a pause.

Lancelot!

DONKEY: Hee-haw!

The DONKEY *lets out a braying laugh.*

Hee-haw! Hee-haw!

The palace gates fly open. In the fire and smoke which pours out three gigantic heads are dimly visible, then occasionally some huge paws, or flashing eyes.

DRAGON: Lancelot! Admire me before we begin to fight! Where are you?

HENRY *rushes out into the square, looking for* LANCELOT; *he even looks down the well.*

Where is he?

HENRY: He's hidden himself, Your Excellency.

DRAGON: Hey, Lancelot. Where are you?

There is the sound of a sword blow. The DRAGON *recoils.*

Who dared to hit me?

LANCELOT (*voice*): It is I – Lancelot!

Complete fog darkens the air. There are threatening roars, and flashes of light. HENRY *dashes into the Town Hall, while the sounds of battle continue.*

MR CAT: Let's run for cover.

DONKEY: It's high time.

They run out. The square fills with people. They are unusually quiet. They whisper among themselves and keep looking at the sky.

FIRST CITIZEN: How painfully the fight drags on.

SECOND CITIZEN: Yes! Two minutes have passed and there is no result as yet.

FIRST CITIZEN: I hope it will all be over immediately.

SECOND CITIZEN: Oh, we were living along so quietly. . . . Here it is time for lunch and I have no appetite. How dreadful! How do you do, Master Gardener. Why do you look so sad?

GARDENER: My tea roses blossomed today as well as my bread roses and my wine roses. You look at them and they fill you up and make you drunk. Sir Dragon promised to drop in to see them and give me money for further experiments. And now he is gone off fighting. Because of this horrible affair, the fruits of many years of my labour may be lost.

PEDDLER (*in a cheerful whisper*): Anyone like some smoked glasses? You look through them and you'll see the Dragon all smoked.

Quiet laughter ripples through the crowd.

FIRST CITIZEN: What effrontery! Ha, ha, ha!

SECOND CITIZEN: See him smoked, well I never!

They all buy glasses.

BOY: Mama, what's the Dragon running away from, all over the sky?

THE CROWD: Shush!

FIRST CITIZEN: He's not running away, boy, he's just manœuvring.

BOY: Why is he drawing in his tail?

THE CROWD: Shush!

FIRST CITIZEN: His tail is drawn in in connection with a previously prepared plan.

FIRST WOMAN CITIZEN: Just think! The fight has been going on for all of six minutes and no end is in sight. Even the simple tradespeople have tripled the price of milk.

SECOND WOMAN CITIZEN: Tradespeople? That's nothing. On my way here I saw a sight that would make your blood run cold. I saw Sugar and Cream, pale as death, rushing out of the shops to the warehouses. Such nervous products! As soon as they hear of a battle they go into hiding.

The CROWD *shies off to one side of the square as* CHARLEMAGNE *enters.*

CHARLEMAGNE: Good day to you, ladies and gentlemen!

This is met with silence.

Don't you recognize me?

FIRST CITIZEN: Of course not. Since yesterday you have become completely unrecognizable.

CHARLEMAGNE: In what way?

GARDENER: You've turned into one of those horrid people. You take in strangers. You ruin the Dragon's temper. That's worse than stepping on the grass. And then you ask in what way . . .

SECOND CITIZEN: Personally I stopped recognizing you altogether after the guard was set up at your house.

CHARLEMAGNE: Yes, that is a shame, isn't it? That stupid guard won't even let me see my own daughter. He says the Dragon gave orders that no one is to go near Elsa.

FIRST CITIZEN: What of it? From his point of view he is quite right.

CHARLEMAGNE: Elsa is all alone there. To be sure she nodded gaily enough to me from the window but she probably only did so to cheer me up. Oh, I am so upset!

SECOND CITIZEN: You're upset? Does that mean you've lost your job as Keeper of the Records?

CHARLEMAGNE: Oh, no.

SECOND CITIZEN: Then what are you talking about?

CHARLEMAGNE: You mean, you don't understand me?

FIRST CITIZEN: No. Since you made friends with that crack-pot Lancelot we don't speak the same language any more.

The sounds of battle increase. The blows from a sword resound.

BOY (*pointing to the sky*): Mama! Mama! He's turned over, with his paws in the air. Someone is striking him so that sparks fly!

CROWD: Shush!

There is a blare of trumpets. HENRY *and the* BURGOMASTER *enter.*

BURGOMASTER: Hear the edict: To avoid an epidemic of eye trouble, and for this reason only, it is forbidden to look at the sky. A communique will advise you of what is transpiring in the sky and it will be issued when necessary by the personal secretary of his Excellency the Dragon.

FIRST CITIZEN: That's only right and proper.

SECOND CITIZEN: High time.

BOY: Mama, why is it bad for my eyes to see how he is being beaten?

CROWD: Hush!

ELSA'S GIRL FRIENDS *enter.*

FIRST GIRL FRIEND: The battle has lasted for ten minutes! Why doesn't that Lancelot surrender?

SECOND GIRL FRIEND: He surely knows he cannot conquer the Dragon.

THIRD GIRL FRIEND: He's just keeping us on tenter-hooks on purpose.

FIRST GIRL FRIEND: I left my gloves at Elsa's, but I don't care now. I am so tired of this fight that I don't care about anything.

SECOND GIRL FRIEND: I haven't any feelings left either. Elsa wanted to give me her new slippers as a souvenir, but I've already forgotten about them.

THIRD GIRL FRIEND: Just think! If it weren't for this stranger the Dragon would have taken Elsa away long since. And we'd be sitting quietly at home weeping.

PEDDLER (*in a cheerful whisper*): Now here's an interesting little scientific instrument. It's a so-called mirror; you look down into it, but see, there's the sky! For a small amount anyone can see the Dragon at one's feet.

There is subdued laughter.

FIRST CITIZEN: What effrontery! Ha, ha, ha!

SECOND CITIZEN: See him at one's feet! As if that could happen!

The mirrors are all snapped up. Everyone in groups looks into them. The sounds of battle are intensified.

FIRST WOMAN CITIZEN: But this is dreadful!

SECOND WOMAN CITIZEN: The poor Dragon!

FIRST WOMAN CITIZEN: He has stopped breathing fire.

SECOND WOMAN CITIZEN: Yes, he's only smoking now.

FIRST CITIZEN: What complicated manœuvres.

SECOND CITIZEN: If you ask me . . . No, I shan't say anything.

FIRST CITIZEN: I don't understand what's going on.

HENRY: Listen to the communiqué of the Municipal

Board of Self-Government: The fight is drawing to its close. The challenger has lost his sword. His lance is broken. Moths have been discovered in the Flying Carpet and they are speedily destroying the enemy's flight potential. Separated from his base the enemy is unable to obtain camphor balls or to use his hands to catch the moths because he has to use them for manœuvrability. Sir Dragon does not destroy his enemy out of sheer love of battle. He is not yet sated with his own prodigious feats nor has he enjoyed to the full his own marvellous courage.

FIRST CITIZEN: Now I understand everything.

BOY: But, Mama, look, there's really someone hacking at his neck!

FIRST CITIZEN: He has three necks, my boy.

BOY: Yes, and now he's getting it in all three necks.

FIRST CITIZEN: That is an optical delusion, I mean illusion.

BOY: That's what I'm saying, it's all a delusion. When I am fighting I know who's on top! Ow, what's that?

FIRST CITIZEN: Take that little squirt away.

SECOND CITIZEN: I don't believe, I can't believe my own eyes! An eye doctor, quickly; get me an eye doctor!

FIRST CITIZEN: It's falling straight down on us. I can't bear it! Don't crowd! Let's see!

One of the DRAGON's *heads crashes noisily into the square.*

BURGOMASTER: A communique! I'd give half my life for a communique!

HENRY: Listen to the communique of the Municipal Board of Self-Government! The enfeebled enemy

Lancelot has lost everything and has been partially taken prisoner.

BOY: What's partially prisoner?

HENRY: Just what I say. It's – a military secret. His remaining parts are still resisting in a state of disorganization. Meantime, Sir Dragon has relieved one of his heads from military service on grounds of health and has put it on the preferred list in the reserves.

BOY: But I still don't understand . . .

FIRST CITIZEN: What don't you understand? Didn't you lose your baby teeth?

BOY: I did.

FIRST CITIZEN: All right then. You get on all right without them.

BOY: But I never lost my head.

FIRST CITIZEN: As if that mattered!

BURGOMASTER: Listen to the review of events to date: To begin with: How can two actually be greater than three? Two heads sit on two necks. . . . That makes four. That's right. And besides they are indestructible.

A second head catapults down into the square.

This review has been postponed for technical reasons. Listen to the communique! Military action is proceeding in accordance with plans drawn up by Sir Dragon.

BOY: Is that all he has to say?

HENRY: For the time being.

FIRST CITIZEN: I have lost two-thirds of my respect for the Dragon. Mr Charlemagne, my dear friend! Why are you standing there all alone?

SECOND CITIZEN: Come over and join us.

FIRST CITIZEN: Will the guard really not let you go near your only daughter? What a shame!

SECOND CITIZEN: Why are you silent?

FIRST CITIZEN: You aren't offended with us, are you?

CHARLEMAGNE: No, I just can't get my bearings. First you frankly did not know me although I knew you. Now you are just as frankly glad to see me.

GARDENER: Ah, Mr Charlemagne, must you remember everything? . . . It's really terrible to think of all the time I lost running to lick the paws of that now one-headed monster. Think of all the flowers I could have raised!

HENRY: Listen to a review of events!

GARDENER: Oh, leave us alone. We're fed up.

BURGOMASTER: We are at war. You must have patience. So I shall begin. There is one God, one sun, one moon, and there is one head on the shoulders of our ruler. To have only one head – that is human, it is humane in the highest sense of the word. Besides, it is highly convenient from the purely military point of view. It palpably narrows the front. To defend one head is three times as easy as to defend three.

The DRAGON's *third head crashes into the square. There is a great outcry. Now people begin to speak in loud voices.*

FIRST CITIZEN: Away with the Dragon!

SECOND CITIZEN: We've been tricked all our lives!

FIRST WOMAN CITIZEN: How wonderful! No one to submit to!

SECOND WOMAN CITIZEN: I feel as though I were drunk! Really I do.

BOY: Mama, now there surely won't be any school? Hooray!

PEDDLER: Who wants a toy? A dragon's head – now you see it – now you don't?

The CROWD *roars with laughter.*

GARDENER: Very smart! And now with a dragon for tree root feeding I can sit in the park! All my life! Never leave it! Hooray!

CROWD: Hooray! Take him away, the old Dra-Dra-Dragon. Give him a whack!

HENRY: Listen to the communique!

CROWD: No we won't! If we want to shout, we'll shout. If we want to bark, we'll bark. How wonderful! Whack him!

BURGOMASTER: Ho there, guard!

The GUARD *runs into the square.*

To HENRY.

Go on speaking. Take it easy at first and then rap their knuckles. Attention!

The CROWD *is silenced.*

HENRY (*very gently*): Just listen, please, to the communique. On all the fronts nothing, literally nothing of interest has occurred. Everything is under satisfactory control. A state of siege is being proclaimed. If there is any rumour-mongering –

He speaks threateningly.

heads will fall – no fines in place of it. Understand? And now go to your homes! Guard, clear the square.

The square is emptied.

Well, how did you like that spectacle?

BURGOMASTER: Better keep quiet, sonny.

HENRY: Why are you smiling?

BURGOMASTER: Hush, sonny.

There is a dull heavy thud which makes the earth tremble.

That's the body of the Dragon which hurtled to the ground near the windmill.

DRAGON'S NUMBER ONE HEAD: Hey, boy!

HENRY: Why are you rubbing your hands, Papa?

BURGOMASTER: Why, my son, the power has just fallen into my hands of its own accord!

NUMBER TWO HEAD: Burgomaster, come here to me! Give me water, Burgomaster.

BURGOMASTER: Everything is going splendidly, Henry. Their late master trained them so well that they will stay right on in the shafts, to haul whoever picks up the reins.

HENRY: But just now, right here in the square . . .

BURGOMASTER: Oh, that was a lot of nonsense. Every dog jumps like mad when you let it off the leash but then it runs of its own free will into its kennel.

NUMBER THREE HEAD: Boy! Come here, I'm dying.

HENRY: And you're not afraid of Lancelot, Papa?

BURGOMASTER: No, my boy. Do you think it was an easy job to kill the Dragon? Probably Sir Lancelot is lying all exhausted on the Flying Carpet and the wind is carrying him away from our city.

HENRY: But if he should suddenly descend on us?

BURGOMASTER: We shall be able to handle him very easily. He has no strength left, I assure you. Our dear old Dragon knew how to put up a good fight. Let's go in now and draw up the first orders. The main thing is to act as if nothing had happened.

NUMBER ONE DRAGON HEAD: Boy! Burgomaster!

BURGOMASTER: Come along, come along. We have no time to waste.

They go into the palace.

NUMBER ONE HEAD: Why, oh, why did I strike him with my second left paw? I should have used my second right one.

NUMBER TWO HEAD: Hey there! Anybody! Is that you, Henry? You kissed my hand yesterday when we met. Hey, you, Citizen! You made me a present of a pipe with three mouthpieces and an inscription: 'Forever Thine.' Where are you, Anna-Maria-Frederika? You said you were in love with me and wore a paring of one of my claws in a little velvet bag around your neck. We have always understood each other. Where are you all? Give me some water. There's the well, right there. Just a swallow! Half a swallow! At least let me moisten my lips.

NUMBER ONE HEAD: Let me, oh, let me begin back at the beginning! I'll crush the life out of every last one of you!

NUMBER TWO HEAD: Just a drop, anyone.

NUMBER THREE HEAD: I should have at least one truly loyal follower, but I never thought of that.

NUMBER TWO HEAD: Hush! There's a live creature near. He's coming. Give me some water.

LANCELOT (*offstage*): I haven't the strength.

LANCELOT *enters the square. He is carrying the Flying Carpet rolled up and his bent sword. He holds the Cap of Invisibility in his hands. The musical instrument is hung over his shoulder. Painfully he gets the dipper at the well and fills it.*

NUMBER ONE HEAD: Your victory was accidental. If I had only used my second right paw. . . .

With difficulty LANCELOT *gives each head a drink.*

NUMBER TWO HEAD: Well, anyhow, farewell!

NUMBER THREE HEAD: I am consoled by the fact that I am leaving you burnt out souls, souls riddled with holes, dead souls. . . . And anyhow, farewell!

NUMBER TWO HEAD: The one person near me as I die is the very one who killed me. That's how life ends!

ALL THREE HEADS (*in chorus*): Life is ended! Farewell!

They fall back.

LANCELOT: He has died, and I am not feeling quite right myself. My arms do not obey me. I can scarcely see. And I keep hearing a voice calling, 'Lancelot! Lancelot!' It's a familiar voice. A deep voice. But I don't want to go. Perhaps I must this time. What do you think, am I dying?

The musical instrument plays a mournful phrase.

Yes, to listen to you that all sounds very edifying and noble. But I feel so ill. I am mortally wounded. Wait wait. . . . But the Dragon is slain, now I can breathe more easily. Nevertheless I shall probably never see you again, Elsa. You will not smile on me, or kiss me or ask: What's the matter with you, Lancelot? Why are you so downcast? Why is your head swimming so? Why do your shoulders ache? Who is calling you so persistently: Lancelot! Lancelot!? It is Death that is calling me, Elsa. I am dying. That is very said, isn't it?

The musical instrument repeats the phrase.

It is very distressing. They have all hidden themselves. What appeared to be a victory – is turned into some kind of a calamity. But you must wait a bit, Death.

You know me. I have looked you in the face more than once and I have never hidden from you. No, I will not come to you. Yes, I hear. Let me think for a moment. They have all hidden themselves, that's what it is. But now, in their homes, they are quietly coming to their senses. Their souls are reviving. Why, they whisper, did we ever feed and pet that monster? For our sakes there's a man who is dying out there in the square, all alone. But now we shall know better! Think of the battle which raged through the sky for our sakes. Think of poor Lancelot who is breathing so hard. No, that is enough. It was because of our weakness that our strongest, kindest, most impatient people were all destroyed. Even stones would have more sense than we have shown. And yet we are human beings. That's what they are whispering right now in every house, in every room. Do you hear?

The musical instrument replies.

Yes, that's just it. That means I am not dying in vain. Farewell, Elsa. I knew that I would love you all my life . . . but I did not believe my life would be ended so soon. Farewell, city, farewell morning, day, evening. Now night is come. . . . Death calls, he is hurrying me. . . . My thoughts are confused. . . . I didn't finish what I was saying. . . . Ho there, you! Do not be afraid! This you can do: You can have pity on each other. Don't be afraid. Love one another and you will be happy! This is the truth, the purest truth on earth. That is all. Now I am going away. Farewell.

The musical instrument echoes.

CURTAIN

ACT THREE

The scene is laid in a luxuriously furnished apartment in the palace of the Burgomaster. On either side of the door at the back of the stage there is a semi-round table laid for supper. In the centre is a medium-sized table. On it lies a thick volume in gold binding.

To one side is a large throne-like chair with a curtain behind it. Opposite it is a window. When the curtain rises an orchestra is playing loudly. A group of citizens, with their eyes fixed on one of the doors, is rehearsing a speech.

CITIZENS (*in a low voice*): One, two, three
    Loudly.
Hail to the Conqueror of the Dragon!
    In a low voice.
One, two, three
    Loudly.
Hail to our Ruler!
    In a low voice.
One, two, three
    Loudly.
Our happiness is so great, it is inconceivable!
    In a low voice.
One, two, three
    Loudly.

We hear footsteps!

Enter HENRY.

Loudly but with calculated timing.

Hurrah! Hurrah! Hurrah!

FIRST CITIZEN: Oh, our Glorious Liberator! Exactly a year ago that cursed, hateful, revolting Dragon was destroyed by you.

CITIZENS: Hurrah Hurrah! Hurrah!

FIRST CITIZEN: Since then we have been very well off. We . . .

HENRY: Just a moment, my friend. Put the accent on 'very'.

FIRST CITIZEN: Yes, sir. Since then we have been v-v-very well off.

HENRY: No, no, my dear man. That's not the way. You mustn't stress the 'v'. That makes you sound as though you were hesitating, stuttering. Stress the 'r'.

FIRST CITIZEN: Since then we have been ver-r-ry well off.

HENRY: That's it. I approve. You see, you know the Conqueror of the Dragon. He is such a simple, even naïve man. He loves sincerity, heartiness. Go on.

FIRST CITIZEN: We don't know what to do with ourselves, we are so happy.

HENRY: That's fine! But wait a minute. Let's put something in there, something like . . . kindness, virtue. The Conqueror of the Dragon loves kindness, virtue.

He snaps his fingers.

Wait, wait! Just a moment. There! I have it! Even the birds chirp more cheerily now that evil is banished and good reigns. Cheep-cheep-chirp – hurrah! There, now let's go over it again.

FIRST CITIZEN: Even the little birdies chirp more cheerily. Evil is banished – good reigns, cheep-cheep-chirp – hurrah!

HENRY: Your chirp is too drab, my good man. See to it your cheep doesn't become a chop or you get it in the neck.

FIRST CITIZEN: Cheep-cheep-chirp! Chirp – hurrah!

HENRY: That's better. Yes, that's good enough. We've already rehearsed the rest, haven't we?

CITIZENS: Yes, Sir Burgomaster, we have.

HENRY: Very good. In a moment the Conqueror of the Dragon, the President of your Free City, will appear before you. Remember, you must all speak in close unison but with warm, humane, democratic feelings. It was the Dragon that insisted on ceremony but we . . .

SENTRY (*from the central door upstage*): Atten-tion! Eyes on the door! His Excellency the President of the Free City is coming along the corridor.

Woodenly, without any expression, in a bass voice.

Oh, you angel! Oh, you benefactor! Killed the Dragon! Just think of it!

There is a blare of music. Enter the BURGOMASTER.

HENRY: Your Excellency, Mr President of the Free City! While I have been on duty there have been no incidents! I have on hand here ten people. Out of the ten, all are unbelievably happy. . . . In the suburbs . . .

BURGOMASTER: At ease, at ease, gentlemen. How do you do, Burgomaster.

He shakes HENRY's *hand.*

Who are you? Oh, the Burgomaster?

HENRY: Our fellow citizens were just recalling the fact

that exactly a year ago you slew the Dragon. They have hurried here to offer you their congratulations.

BURGOMASTER: You don't say! What a pleasant surprise. Well, well, out with it.

CITIZENS (*in low tones*): One, two, three
Loudly.

Hail to the Conqueror of the Dragon!
In low tones.

One, two, three
Loudly.

Hail to our Ruler. . . .
Enter the JAILER.

BURGOMASTER: Stop! Stop! How do you do, Jailer?

JAILER: Good day to you, Your Excellency.

BURGOMASTER (*to the citizens*): Thank you, gentlemen: I already know everything that you were preparing to say to me. Oh, dammit, an unwanted tear!
He wipes his eyes.

But you know we are having a wedding and I still have a few little things to attend to. So run along now and then come back to the wedding. We'll have a jolly time. The nightmare is behind us, we can begin to live. Am I right?

CITIZENS: Hip, hip, hooray!

BURGOMASTER: That's what I like to hear! Slavery is nothing more than a legend. We have been re-born. Do you remember what I was like in the days of the cursed Dragon? I was sick, I was crazy. And now? I am sound as a cucumber. I do not even need to speak about you. You are always gay and happy as larks. So now fly away! Hurray! Henry, show them out!
The CITIZENS *leave.*

Now, Jailer, what's going on in your bailiwick?

JAILER: The prisoners are locked up.

BURGOMASTER: And how's my former assistant?

JAILER: He's having a horrible time.

BURGOMASTER: Ha, ha! I bet you're lying.

JAILER: No, honestly, he is having a horrible time.

BURGOMASTER: What do you mean by that?

JAILER: Well, he is frantic.

BURGOMASTER: Ha, ha! That's just as it should be! A revolting personality. There used to be times when I was telling an anecdote, all the others would laugh, but he would say it was so old it had a beard. So let him lie in prison. Did you show him a picture of me?

JAILER: I certainly did.

BURGOMASTER: Which one? The one where I am happy smiles all over?

JAILER: That's the very one.

BURGOMASTER: What happened?

JAILER: He cried.

BURGOMASTER: No doubt you're lying.

JAILER: Honestly, he cried.

BURGOMASTER: Ha, ha! That's nice. What about the weavers who furnished that fellow . . . with the Flying Carpet?

JAILER: They are a pain in the neck, the devils. They are put on different floors but they stick together as one man. What one of them says, the other says.

BURGOMASTER: But have they at least lost weight?

JAILER: Everyone loses weight in my place.

BURGOMASTER: And the blacksmith?

JAILER: He has sawed through his bars again. We have

F

had to put bars made of diamonds in the windows of his cell.

BURGOMASTER: Good, good. Don't spare any expense. How's he behaving now?

JAILER: He's puzzled.

BURGOMASTER: Ha, ha! That suits me!

JAILER: The Master Hatmaker has made such pretty caps for the mice the cats don't touch them.

BURGOMASTER: They don't? Why?

JAILER: Because they are lost in admiration. As for the musician, he sings. It's very depressing. When I go to see him I put wax in my ears.

BURGOMASTER: That's all good news. Now what about the city?

JAILER: It's quiet. But people are writing.

BURGOMASTER: Writing what?

JAILER: They are writing the letter 'L' on the walls. That means Lancelot.

BURGOMASTER: Nonsense. The letter 'L' stands for '*Love* for the President'.

JAILER: I see. So I don't need to arrest those who write it?

BURGOMASTER: No! Why not arrest them? What else do they write?

JAILER: I am ashamed to tell you. 'The President is a beast.' 'His son – is a scoundrel. . . . The President . . .'
He giggles in a bass voice.
No, I don't dare repeat it, not the way they express themselves. But most of all they write the letter 'L'.

BURGOMASTER: The fools! They were taken in by that Lancelot. By the way, is there still no news of him?

JAILER: He vanished.

BURGOMASTER: Have you asked the birds?

JAILER: Yes.

BURGOMASTER: All of them?

JAILER: Yes. O yes, the eagle gave me a message from them. Pecked it into my ear.

BURGOMASTER: Well, what did it say?

JAILER: They say they have not seen Lancelot. Only one parrot was affirmative. When you ask him: Seen him? He answers: Seen him. You ask: Lancelot? He answers: Lancelot. But everyone knows what kind of a bird a parrot is.

BURGOMASTER: What about the snakes?

JAILER: They'd have crawled into town themselves if they had heard anything. They're our friends. After all they are connections of the late lamented. But they haven't come around.

BURGOMASTER: And the fishes?

JAILER: Not a word out of them.

BURGOMASTER: Do you think they know anything?

JAILER: No. The learned pisciculturists have looked them straight in the eye and they confirm this; they don't know a thing. In short, Lancelot, alias St George, alias Perseus the Adventurer – he's called something different in every country – has not been discovered anywhere.

BURGOMASTER: Well then, let him go to hell.

HENRY *enters.*

HENRY: The father of the happy bride has arrived, Charlemagne, Keeper of the Records.

BURGOMASTER: Aha! Aha! I want very much to see him. Ask him in.

CHARLEMAGNE *comes through the doors hesitantly.*

You can run along, Jailer. Keep up the good work. I
am pleased with you.

JAILER: We aim to please.

BURGOMASTER: Go on aiming. Charlemagne, are you
acquainted with our Jailer?

CHARLEMAGNE: Only slightly, Mr President.

BURGOMASTER: Well, never mind. Perhaps you'll get
to know him better.

JAILER: Shall I take him along?

BURGOMASTER: You want to grab everyone right off!
No, no, go along for now. See you soon.

The JAILER *leaves.*

Well now, Charlemagne, you no doubt guess why
we sent for you? All sorts of government worries and
problems have prevented my dropping by to see you
myself. But you and Elsa know about the orders that
have been put up all over the city and that this is the
day of the wedding.

CHARLEMAGNE: Yes, Mr President, we know about it.

BURGOMASTER: We government people do not have
the time to call with a bunch of flowers, make a pro-
posal, or moon around sighing. We do not propose,
we merely proclaim our intentions. Ha, ha! It's very
convenient. Is Elsa happy?

CHARLEMAGNE: No.

BURGOMASTER: Indeed! Of course she is happy. What
about you?

CHARLEMAGNE: I am in despair, Mr President.

BURGOMASTER: What ingratitude! I slew the
Dragon . . .

CHARLEMAGNE: You must excuse me, Mr President,
but I cannot believe that.

BURGOMASTER: Oh, yes you can!

CHARLEMAGNE: I give you my word! I cannot do it.

BURGOMASTER: You can, you can. If I can believe it myself, you can do so even far more easily.

CHARLEMAGNE: No.

HENRY: He simply doesn't want to.

BURGOMASTER: But why?

HENRY: He's just raising objections.

BURGOMASTER: Very well then. I offer you the post of my first assistant.

CHARLEMAGNE: I don't want it.

BURGOMASTER: Nonsense. You do want it.

CHARLEMAGNE: No.

BURGOMASTER: Stop this bargaining. I have no time for it. You will have a government house near the park, not far from the market, with a hundred and fifty-three rooms, with all the windows facing south. Your salary will be fabulous. Besides, every time you come to your office you will get travelling expenses, and whenever you go home you will get a severance allowance. If you dine out you'll do so on an official expense account, but if you stay at home you will be given an in-residence allowance. You will be almost as wealthy as I am. That's all. You agree to it?

CHARLEMAGNE: No.

BURGOMASTER: Then what do you want?

CHARLEMAGNE: We ask only one thing, Mr President. Leave us alone.

BURGOMASTER: That's fine – leave you alone! But if I don't choose to? Besides from the government's point of view the thing has a sound basis. The Conqueror of the Dragon marries the girl whom he rescued. It sounds so convincing. Can't you see that?

CHARLEMAGNE: Why do you torture us? I've only just taught myself to think, Mr President, and that in itself was torture enough, but now there's this wedding. Why I could easily lose my mind.

BURGOMASTER: You mustn't! You mustn't! All these mental diseases are sheer psychiatric inventions.

CHARLEMAGNE: Good God! How helpless we are! The very fact that our city is as hushed and subservient as it was before – it's all so terrifying.

BURGOMASTER: What's all this delirium? What's terrifying? What are you and your daughter trying to do – mutiny?

CHARLEMAGNE: No. We took a long walk in the woods today and talked everything over very carefully. Tomorrow when she will no longer be alive I too will die.

BURGOMASTER: What do you mean – not alive? What sort of nonsense is this?

CHARLEMAGNE: Do you really think she would survive this wedding?

BURGOMASTER: Of course I do. It will be a fine and merry holiday. Any other man would be delighted to marry off his daughter to such a wealthy bridegroom.

HENRY: And he too is really delighted.

CHARLEMAGNE: No. I am an elderly and courteous gentleman. It is very difficult for me to say this to your face, but still I will say it: this wedding is a calamity for us.

HENRY: What a boring method of bargaining.

BURGOMASTER: Now listen, my dear man. I am not going to offer you any more than I have already. You evidently want shares in our enterprises too. But you shan't get them! Whatever the Dragon so brazenly accumulated is now in the hands of the best people in town. To state it baldly, in my hands and partly in Henry's. This is all perfectly legal.

CHARLEMAGNE: Of course. You make the laws.

BURGOMASTER: You may go. But remember this: First, at the wedding you will see to it that you are jolly, full of fun and witty. Second, there are to be no deaths! Kindly continue to exist as long as I find it convenient for you to do so. Tell your daughter this too. Third, in the future, you will address me as 'Your Excellency'. Do you see this list? There are fifty families here. All your best friends. If you make any trouble, all these fifty hostages will disappear and not leave a trace behind. Now go along. No, wait. A coach will be sent for you immediately. You will transport your daughter here to the palace and no monkey business! Understand?

CHARLEMAGNE (exits): Now everything will go as smooth as silk.

HENRY: What did the Jailer report?

BURGOMASTER: There is not a cloud in the sky.

HENRY: And what about those 'Ls'?

BURGOMASTER: Oh well, weren't there a lot of things scribbled on the walls in the Dragon's time? Let them scribble. It seems to console them and it does us no harm. Just tell me, is this armchair empty?

HENRY (feeling the chair): Oh, Papa! There isn't anyone in it. Sit down.

BURGOMASTER: Don't smile. In his Cap of Invisibility he could get in anywhere.

HENRY: Papa, you don't know that man. He is crammed to the gills with prejudices. His knightly courtesy would require him, before he entered a house, to remove his cap – and then the guard would seize him.

BURGOMASTER: But in a year's time his character may have deteriorated.

He sits down.

And now, my boy, let us talk about our own affairs. There is the matter of a small debt you owe me, my bright lad.

HENRY: What debt, Papa?

BURGOMASTER: You bribed my three footmen to spy on me, read my papers, et cetera. Isn't that so?

HENRY: Whatever are you talking about, Papa!

BURGOMASTER: Just wait, my boy, and don't interrupt. I raised their wages five hundred crowns out of my own pocket, to see that they only reported to you what I allowed them to. Therefore you owe me five hundred crowns, you young scamp.

HENRY: No, Papa. When I found out what you had done I raised them to six hundred.

BURGOMASTER: And I, sensing that, I went up to one thousand, you little pig! Therefore the balance is in my favour. So don't raise them any more, my sweet son. On the wages they already receive they have been over-eating, getting dissipated and running wild. If you don't watch out they will fall on us. It will be necessary for you to extricate my private secretary. It became necessary to send the poor fellow to a psychiatric hospital.

HENRY: You don't say! Why?

BURGOMASTER: You see, you and I bribed and counter-bribed him so many times a day that he now can't think who his master really is. He was carrying tales about me to me. He was plotting against himself, in order to wangle his own job for himself. He's an honest fellow, hard-working; it's sad to see how he is tormenting himself. Let's go and visit him in the hospital tomorrow and straighten him out, at long last, as to who his employer is. Ah, my son! You're my fine boy! And so you wanted to get into your Papa's shoes. . . .

HENRY: Whatever are you talking about?

BURGOMASTER: None of that, my little one! This is a matter of common sense. Do you know what I propose? Let's watch each other, but keep it in the family, as father and son, without all the outsiders. We'd save a whale of a lot of money.

HENRY: Why, Papa, what's money?

BURGOMASTER: Indeed what is it. When you die you can't take it with you. . . .

There is a sound of horses' hoofs and bells.

He rushes to the window.

She has arrived! Our beauty has come! What a coach! How marvellous! It is all decorated with a dragon's scales. And there is Elsa herself! She's a wonder! All in velvet. Power really is a fine thing to have.

Then he whispers.

You will question her?

HENRY: Whom?

BURGOMASTER: Elsa. She's been so silent all these last days. Ask her if she doesn't know where . . .

He looks around.

Lancelot is. Question her cautiously. And I'll listen from behind the curtain.

He hides. Enter ELSA *and* CHARLEMAGNE.

HENRY: Elsa, I greet you. You are getting prettier every day and that's very sweet of you. The President is changing his clothes. He asked me to make his excuses. Have a seat in the armchair, Elsa.

He seats her with her back to the curtain hiding the BURGOMASTER.

And you can wait in the vestibule, Charlemagne.

CHARLEMAGNE (*bows and leaves*): Elsa, I am very pleased that the President is getting into his regalia. I have wanted for a long time to have a private chat with you, just a friendly heart to heart talk. Why do you not speak? Eh? Don't you wish to reply? I am devoted to you, in my own way, you know. Speak to me.

ELSA: About what?

HENRY: Anything you like.

ELSA: I don't know . . . I don't want to say anything.

HENRY: That's not possible. Today is your wedding day. . . . Oh, Elsa . . . Again I must give you up. But the Conqueror of the Dragon is still the Conqueror. I'm a cynic. I make fun of everyone, but to him I have to bow. You're not listening?

ELSA: No, I'm not.

HENRY: Can it be that I am a stranger to you? We were such friends, since we were infants. Do you remember when you had the measles and I kept coming to your window until I came down with them myself? Then you visited me and wept because I was so sick and listless. Remember?

ELSA: Yes.

HENRY: Can it be that the children which we once were have suddenly passed away? Has nothing of them remained in either you or me? Come on, let's talk together as we used to do, like brother and sister.

ELSA: Very well, let's.

The BURGOMASTER *peeks out from behind the curtain and makes a gesture of applause to* HENRY.

Do you want to know why I have been silent all this while?

The BURGOMASTER *nods.*

Because I am afraid.

HENRY: Of whom?

ELSA: Of people.

HENRY: Really? Tell me just which people you fear. We'll clap them into jail and you will feel easier at once.

The BURGOMASTER *takes out his notebook.*

Well, tell me their names.

ELSA: No, Henry, that wouldn't help.

HENRY: It would help, I assure you. I have tried it out myself. Your sleep, your appetite, your mood — everything will improve.

ELSA: But, do you see. . . . I don't know how to explain it to you. . . . I am afraid of everybody.

HENRY: So that's it. . . . I understand. I understand it very well. Everybody, including me, seems cruel to you? Is that right? Perhaps you won't believe me but I myself am afraid of them. I am afraid of my father.

The BURGOMASTER *throws up his hands in a gesture of dismay.*

I am afraid of our trusted servants. And I pretend to be cruel so as to make them fear me. Alas, we are all caught in our own webs. But go on, tell me some more, I am listening.

The BURGOMASTER *nods approvingly.*

ELSA: Well, what else can I tell you. . . . First I was angry, then I grieved, and then I became quite indifferent. I am more submissive now than I ever was. Anything at all can be done with me now.

The BURGOMASTER *giggles out loud, then alarmed at himself he hides again behind the curtain.* ELSA *looks around.*

Who was that?

HENRY: Pay no attention. They're getting ready for the wedding feast in there. My poor, dear little sister. What a pity that Lancelot disappeared, disappeared without leaving a single trace. I have only just come to understand him. He was an astonishing man. We were very guilty in his sight. Is there really no hope of his coming back?

The BURGOMASTER *slips out from behind the curtain. He is all attention.*

ELSA: He . . . he will not return.

HENRY: You mustn't think that. I somehow feel we shall see him again.

ELSA: No.

HENRY: Believe me, Elsa.

ELSA: I like to hear you say it but . . . Can anyone overhear us?

The BURGOMASTER *leans over the back of* ELSA'S *chair.*

HENRY: Of course not, my dear. Today is a holiday. All spies are off duty.

ELSA: You see . . . I know about Lancelot.

HENRY: Don't! Don't tell me if it pains you.

The BURGOMASTER *shakes his fist menacingly at* HENRY.

ELSA: No, I have been silent so long that now I have the urge to tell you everything. No one except me can understand how sad it is and especially in a city like this one where I was born. But you are listening so closely to me today. . . . Well, in short . . . Just a year ago, when the fight ended, Mr Cat rushed over to the Palace Square. There he saw Lancelot, white, white as a ghost, standing among the Dragon's heads. He was leaning on his sword and smiling so as not to upset Mr Cat. Mr Cat then tore over to my house to get help. But the guards were watching me so closely that not a fly could get past them to enter the house. They chased the cat away.

HENRY: The brutes!

ELSA: Then he called his friend the donkey. They laid the wounded man on the donkey's back and took him through little side streets out of the city.

HENRY: Why?

ELSA: Alas, Lancelot was so weak people might easily have killed him. So they took a little trail which led them up into the mountains. Mr Cat remained by his side and kept track of his pulse.

HENRY: It went on beating, I trust?

ELSA: Yes, but fainter and fainter. Then Mr Cat cried:

'Halt' and the donkey stood still. Night had fallen. They were by then high, high up in the mountains, and all around it was so very quiet, and cold. 'You must turn back to the city,' said the cat. 'People cannot harm him any more. Let Elsa say farewell to him and then we shall bury him.'

HENRY: He died, the poor fellow!

ELSA: He died, Henry. But that stubborn donkey said that he refused to turn around. So he went on. But Mr Cat came back. You see he is really very devoted to our house. He came back and told me everything so that I have nothing to hope for. Everything is over for me.

BURGOMASTER: Hooray! It's all over.

He begins to dance all over the room.

It's all over! I am the complete master over everybody! Now there is no one to fear. Thank you, Elsa! This really is a holiday! Who will dare say now that I did not slay the Dragon? Well, *who* dares?

ELSA: Did he hear us?

HENRY: Of course.

ELSA: And you knew it?

HENRY: Oh, Elsa, don't play the naïve girl. You're getting married today.

ELSA: Father! Father!

CHARLEMAGNE *rushes in.*

CHARLEMAGNE: What's the matter with you, my little darling?

He starts to embrace her.

BURGOMASTER: Hands off! You will stand at attention in the presence of my bride!

CHARLEMAGNE (*drawing himself up at attention*): There,

there, calm yourself, don't cry. What can you do?
You can't do anything at all.

Music blares forth.

BURGOMASTER (*runs over to the window*): How fine!
How neighbourly! The guests are arriving for the
wedding. The horses are all decked out with ribbons!
There are little lanterns on the shafts! How wonderful
it is to be alive and know that no fool can interfere
with you. Smile, Elsa. Any second now, at the
appointed time, the President of the Free City will
enclose you in his embrace.

The doors are opened wide.

Welcome, welcome my dear people, my dear guests.

The guests enter. They come up in pairs past ELSA *and
the* BURGOMASTER. *They speak formally, almost in a
whisper.*

FIRST CITIZEN: Our congratulations to the bride and to
the groom. Everyone is very happy.

SECOND CITIZEN: All the houses are decorated with
lanterns.

FIRST CITIZEN: Outdoors it's as bright as day.

SECOND CITIZEN: All the wine shops are overcrowded.

BOY: They are all cursing and fighting.

GUESTS: Hush!

GARDENER: Allow me to present to you these little
bluebells. To be sure they will toll rather sadly for
you. Never mind, by tomorrow they will have faded
and stopped.

FIRST GIRL FRIEND: Elsa dear, do try to be merry. Or
you'll make me cry and that would spoil the eyelashes I
put on so cleverly for today.

SECOND GIRL FRIEND: After all, he is a cut above the

Dragon. . . . He has arms, legs and no scales. After all, even if he is the President, he is a human being. Tell us all about it tomorrow. It will be so interesting!

THIRD GIRL FRIEND: You will be able to do so much good for people! For instance, you can ask your husband to discharge my father's boss. Then Papa can have his job and will get twice as much salary, and we will be so happy!

BURGOMASTER (*counting the guests under his breath*): One, two, three, four. . .

Then he counts the place settings.

One, two, three. . . . Apparently there is one guest too many. . . . Of course, it's the boy. . . . There now don't howl. You can eat from your mother's plate. Well, we are all here. Ladies and gentlemen, be seated. We shall quickly and informally get through the marriage ceremony and then we shall continue with the wedding feast. I got a fish which was created to be eaten. It smiles with joy when it is being boiled and it tells the cook when it is ready. And there is a turkey stuffed with its own young. Cosy, family style. And these are roast piglets that were not only fed but trained especially for our table. They know how to sit up and beg and to shake hands even when they are roasted. . . . Stop whimpering, boy, it's not terrible at all, it's amusing. And the wines – you know they are so old they have fallen into their second childhood, and are dancing around in their bottles like little tots. The vodka too is distilled to such a degree of purity the carafe seems empty.

He picks up a carafe.

Why look, it really is empty! Those damned footmen

have cleaned the vodka out altogether. Well, never mind, there are a lot more carafes – on the sideboard. How agreeable it is to be rich, ladies and gentlemen! Have you all found your places? That's fine. One moment! Elsa, give me your little paw!

ELSA *holds out her hand to the* BURGOMASTER.

You darling little kitten! You rascal! What a warm little paw! Hold your little chin up! Smile! Is everything ready, Henry?

HENRY: Just so, Mr President.

BURGOMASTER: Proceed.

HENRY: I am a poor speaker, ladies and gentlemen, and I fear that my speech may be a bit muddled. A year ago a self-assured traveller in these parts challenged the cursed Dragon to mortal combat. A special commission, set up by the Municipal Board for Self-Government, established the following: the late brazen challenger did no more than infuriate the late monster and succeeded in wounding him slightly. Whereupon our former Burgomaster and present President of the Free City, heroically attacked the Dragon and slew him, this time for good, after having performed various feats of great courage.

Applause.

The thorny growth of shameful slavery was torn up by the roots out of the harvest of our social crop.

Applause.

The grateful city has reached the following decision: Inasmuch as we used to present our best young maidens to the cursed Monster, we can now do no less than accord those simple and natural rights to our dear Liberator!

G

Applause.

Therefore, to underscore the greatness of our President on the one hand, and the subservience and devotion of the city on the other, I, as Burgomaster, shall now perform the office of marriage. Strike up the organ! The Wedding Hymn!

Organ plays fortissimo.

Clerks! Open the Book of Fortunate Events.

CLERKS (*enter carrying huge fountain pens*): For four hundred years the names of the unfortunate girls doomed to the Dragon have been entered here. Four hundred pages have been filled. As the first on Page four hundred and one we shall inscribe the name of the lucky girl who will take as her bridegroom the courageous Slayer of the Monster.

Applause.

Bridegroom, answer me with a clear conscience: Do you agree to take this maiden to be your wife?

BURGOMASTER: For the good of the city I am prepared to do anything.

Applause.

HENRY (*to the* CLERKS): Write! But be careful! If you make a blot you'll be obliged to lick it up. That's right! . . . Well, that's all. Oh, excuse me, there is still one formality. Bride: Do you consent to be the wife of the President of the Free City?

There is a pause.

Well, answer, do you?

ELSA: No.

HENRY: Very good. Write that she consents.

ELSA: Don't you dare write!

The CLERKS *draw back uncertainly.*

HENRY: Elsa, don't interfere with their work.

BURGOMASTER: But, my dear boy, she's not interfering with them. When a girl says 'no' she means 'yes'. Go on writing!

ELSA: No! I'll tear that page to pieces and stamp on it!

BURGOMASTER: Oh, these charming girlish hesitations, these tears, these illusions. Every girl weeps in her own way before her wedding and then is completely happy afterwards. We shall hold her little hands tight, and do what we will with her. . . .

ELSA: Let me say just one word! Please!

HENRY: Elsa!

BURGOMASTER: Don't shout, my boy. Everything is going as it should. The bride asks to speak. Let her have her say and that will conclude the formalities. There now, it's all right, we're all friends here.

ELSA: My friends! I always thought that you all obeyed only the Dragon. But you, my friends, all turn out to be dragons yourselves. I do not blame you, but I implore you to come to your senses. Will no one stand up for me?

BOY: I would but Mama is holding me back.

BURGOMASTER: Now that's enough. The bride has made her speech. Life will go on as usual, as if nothing had happened.

BOY: Mama!

BURGOMASTER: Shut up, little one. That's enough red tape, Henry. Write down that 'the marriage rite is considered completed' – and let's get on with the eats. I'm awfully hungry.

HENRY (*to the* CLERKS): Set down that the marriage rite

was completed. Well? Hurry up! Have you lost your minds?

The CLERKS *take up their pens. There is a loud knock on the door. The* CLERKS *fall back again.*

BURGOMASTER: Who's there?

Silence.

Hey, you out there! Whoever you are you can apply tomorrow, tomorrow during office hours, to my secretary. I have no time now! I'm getting married! *There is another loud knock.*

Don't open the doors. You clerks, go ahead and write!

The door flies open by itself. There is no one outside.

Henry, come here to me! What does this mean?

HENRY: Oh, Papa, it's the usual thing. The plaints of our maiden here have stirred up all the naïve inhabitants of the rivers, forests, lakes. The goblins from the attics, the water sprites from the wells. . . . Leave them alone. . . . What harm can they do us? They are as invisible and powerless as a so-called conscience and other such things. Well, we may have a bad dream or two – that's all.

BURGOMASTER: No, it is he!

HENRY: Who?

BURGOMASTER: Lancelot. He has on his Cap of Invisibility. He's standing right beside us. He is listening to what we are saying. His sword is hanging over my head.

HENRY: Dearest Papa! If you don't come to your senses I'll take the power into my own hands.

BURGOMASTER: Music! Play! Forgive this little involuntary delay, but I do so hate a draught. It was a draught that opened the doors – that's all. Elsa, my treasure, calm yourself! I am going to proclaim our marriage officially after one last confirmation. What's that? Who's running in here?

A frightened FOOTMAN *rushes in.*

FOOTMAN: Take it back! Take it back!

BURGOMASTER: Take what back?

FOOTMAN: Take back your cursed money! I will not serve you any longer!

BURGOMASTER: Why?

FOOTMAN: He will kill me for all my vileness.

He rushes out.

BURGOMASTER: Who will kill him? Eh? Henry!

A SECOND FOOTMAN *rushes in.*

SECOND FOOTMAN: He's coming down the corridor! I made a low bow to him and he paid no attention to me! He doesn't even look at people now. Ow, ow, we're going to get it for all that we've done. Ow, we'll get it.

He rushes out.

BURGOMASTER: Henry!

HENRY: Behave as if nothing were the matter. No matter what happens. That will save you.

A THIRD FOOTMAN *appears, walking backwards, He speaks to the empty space.*

THIRD FOOTMAN: I can prove it! My wife can confirm it! I always denounced their behaviour! I only took their money for reasons of nervousness. I will testify. . . .

He leaves.

BURGOMASTER: Look!

HENRY: As if nothing were the matter! For God's sake, as if nothing were the matter!

LANCELOT *enters, followed by* MR CAT *who curls himself up in the armchair watching with satisfaction throughout the following.*

BURGOMASTER: Ah, how do you do! You were one person we did not expect. Nevertheless we extend you our welcome. We don't have enough china to go around, but you can eat out of a deep dish and I'll take a shallow one. I'd order some more dishes brought in but my footmen, the idiots, have all run away. . . . And we are just getting married, as it were. He, he, he, and this is a personal, as it were, an intimate matter. Very cosy . . . Allow me to introduce you. . . . Where are the guests? Ah, they have dropped something and are looking for it under the tables. Well, here's my son, Henry. I believe you have already met. He's so very young and already a burgomaster. He has come far since I . . . since we . . . well, anyhow, since the Dragon was slain. What's the matter? Do please come in.

HENRY: Why don't you speak?

BURGOMASTER: Yes indeed, what's the matter? What kind of a trip did you have? What's new? Don't you want to rest after your journey? The guard will show you the way.

LANCELOT: Greetings, Elsa!

ELSA: Lancelot!

She runs over to him.

Is it really you?

LANCELOT: Yes, Elsa.

ELSA: And your hands are warm. And your hair has grown since we saw each other last. Or does it only seem so to me? But your cloak is the same. Lancelot!

She seats him at the small table in the centre of the room.
Take a little wine. Or rather no, don't touch anything
of theirs. You rest a bit and then we'll leave. Father!
He has come. Oh, Father! It's just as it was on that
evening. It's just as it was then when you and I thought
that only one thing remained for us to do – to die
quietly. Lancelot!

LANCELOT: Do you mean you love me as much as
ever?

ELSA: Father, do you hear? How many times have we
dreamed of his coming in and asking: Elsa, do you
love me as much as ever? And my answer is: Yes,
Lancelot! And then I shall ask: Where have you been
for all this long while?

LANCELOT: Far, far away in the Black Mountains.

ELSA: You were very ill?

LANCELOT: Yes, Elsa. I was mortally wounded and that
is very, very dangerous.

ELSA: Who nursed you?

LANCELOT: The wife of a woodchopper. A good kind
woman. Except her feelings were hurt because in my
delirium I kept calling 'Elsa'.

ELSA: You mean you missed me?

LANCELOT: I did.

ELSA: And how I suffered! They tormented me so here.

BURGOMASTER: Who did? Impossible! Why didn't
you complain to us? We would have taken steps!

LANCELOT: I know everything, Elsa.

ELSA: You do?

LANCELOT: Yes.

ELSA: How so?

LANCELOT: In the Black Mountains, not far from the

woodchopper's cottage, there is a huge cave. In the cave there lies the book I told you about, the Book of Wrongs. In it are inscribed all the crimes of the evil-doers, all the woes of their innocent victims.

HENRY *and the* BURGOMASTER *tiptoe towards the door.*

ELSA: Is that where you read about us?

LANCELOT: Yes, Elsa. Hey, you murderers. Don't you dare stir!

BURGOMASTER: Why speak so severely to us?

LANCELOT: Because I am not the man I was a year ago. I freed you then and what have you done?

BURGOMASTER: Oh my God! If you are not satisfied with me I'll go into retirement.

LANCELOT: You are not going anywhere!

HENRY: Quite right. You cannot conceive how he behaved while you were away. I can furnish you with a complete list of his crimes which have not yet been entered in the Book of Wrongs, crimes he had intended to commit.

LANCELOT: Hold your tongue!

HENRY: But, allow me. If you look into things more deeply, I am not guilty of anything. It's the way I was trained.

LANCELOT: Everyone was trained. But why were you the best pupil, you beast?

HENRY: Let's go away, Papa. He's calling me names.

LANCELOT: No, you are not to stir. I have been here for a whole month, Elsa.

ELSA: And you never came to see me!

LANCELOT: Oh yes I did, but in my Cap of Invisibility, early in the morning. I kissed you gently, so that you would not be awakened. I wandered around the town. I saw the terrible life of the people. It's one thing to read about it, but to see it with your own eyes – that's worse. You there!

The FIRST CITIZEN *stands up.*

I saw you weep with pleasure when you yelled: 'Hail to the Conqueror of the Dragon' to the Burgomaster.

FIRST CITIZEN: It's perfectly true I did cry but I was pretending, Sir Lancelot.

LANCELOT: Yet you know that he did not slay the Dragon.

FIRST CITIZEN: When I was in my own home, I knew it . . . but in public . . .

He spread his hands.

LANCELOT: Gardener!

The GARDENER *crawls out from under a table.*

You were teaching snapdragons to say: 'Hurrah for the President?'

GARDENER: I was.

LANCELOT: Did they learn it?

GARDENER: Yes, except that every time they said it they stuck out their tongues at me. I had expected to get money to make new experiments . . . but

LANCELOT: And you down there!

The SECOND CITIZEN *crawls out from under the table.*

When the Burgomaster got angry at you, did he put your only son in the dungeon?

SECOND CITIZEN: Yes. And it was so damp there the boy is still coughing.

LANCELOT: Yet after that you gave the Burgomaster a pipe inscribed with the sentiment: 'Forever thine'?

SECOND CITIZEN: How else could I soften his heart?

LANCELOT: What am I to do with you all?

BURGOMASTER: Let them go. This is not a job for you. Henry and I can handle it all splendidly. That will be the worst punishment for the scum. You take Elsa by the hand and leave us to lead our lives in our own way – the humane and democratic way.

LANCELOT: That I cannot do. Come in now, friends.

Enter the WEAVERS, *the* BLACKSMITH, *the* MASTER HATMAKER, *the* MASTER OF MUSICAL INSTRUMENTS.

You have grievously disappointed me. I thought you could manage without me. Why did you submit and go to prison? There are so many of you!

THE WEAVERS (*together*): He didn't give us time to collect our wits.

LANCELOT: Take these people away – the Burgomaster and the President.

THE WEAVERS (*taking hold of* HENRY *and the* BURGOMASTER): March!

BLACKSMITH: I tested the bars myself. They're strong. March!

MASTER HATMAKER: I used to make magnificent hats, but prison coarsened my taste. March.

MASTER OF MUSICAL INSTRUMENTS: In my cell I fashioned a violin out of black bread and plaited strings out of cobwebs. My violin has only a sad and faint tone and it is you who are to blame. So march to our music.

HENRY: But this is absurd, it's not proper. Things don't happen this way.

THE WEAVERS: March!

BURGOMASTER: I protest, this is inhuman!

THE WEAVERS: March!

Gloomy, simple, barely audible music plays. HENRY *and the* BURGOMASTER *are taken away.*

LANCELOT: Elsa, I am not the person I used to be. Do you see that?

ELSA: Yes, but I love you even more.

LANCELOT: We shall not be able to go away. . . .

ELSA: That makes no difference.

LANCELOT: I have some small jobs to do, but they are difficult ones. In each case I shall have to slay a dragon.

BOY: Will we suffer from this?

LANCELOT: You will not.

FIRST CITIZEN: Will we?

LANCELOT: I am going to have to work with you first. You will all have to have patience. I implore you to be patient. Do some grafting, like a gardener. Pull up the weeds carefully so as not to harm the healthy roots. If you will think about it, you will find that people in reality, perhaps, maybe, with some exceptions, are worth careful cultivation.

MR CAT (*springing up*): That's the truth!

Music is heard.

LANCELOT: Elsa, give me your little . . . give me your hand.

CURTAIN

PRODUCTION NOTES

ANYONE WHO has ever had the job of choosing a school play will know the difficulty of finding something suitable, worthwhile, and original. Here is an exciting new play that gives an opportunity to a young, large cast of presenting a play equally entertaining to their parents as to their schoolfriends and younger brothers and sisters.

The Dragon is a most unusual play by Western standards, and has great dramatic atmosphere. It is a political satire, a fairy tale, and a pantomime. The production of the play can vary greatly according to the interpretation of it, and it gives great scope for staging, costuming, make-up, lighting, and sound effects. But although it could be a very elaborate production it can also be effective presented simply.

Bedminster Down School, Bristol, is a mixed comprehensive school. Before deciding to present this play we read parts of it with different age-groups ranging from twelve to seventeen years. The reaction to the comedy was immediate and enthusiastic. The political allegory was understood, and there was no need to labour it.

The cast can be as large as the producer wishes or can accommodate on stage. There is very good scope for crowd work, and the crowd scenes are very important. As usual, there are too few girls' parts, but we improved the balance by giving Elsa a mother. (Quite a good character can be evolved by selecting the more diffident, conventional-attitude lines written for Charlemagne.) The first and second weavers were played by girls (with some judicious cutting), and the Master Hatmaker became a Milliner. The gardener was played by a girl. And many of the girls in the crowd chose to dress as boys. This play could be equally well done by a boys' school or a girls' school. The play can be cast throughout the school, and need not be limited to the sixth form, although probably older pupils will be needed to play Lancelot, Charlemagne, the Burgomaster, and the Dragon.

The Dragon requires three distinct characterizations which we achieved by casting three boys who were dressed identically. The changeover in Act One on page 13 was made during a blackout. The first character was modelled on the image of a confident, smiling military leader at a May Day parade, complete with bouquet of flowers to present to Elsa with a Russian embrace. The second represents the sinister authority of the secret police. And the third is the old cynic who is contemptuous of the humanity he has destroyed, but knows that now he can only maintain his position by force. They were dressed like the early communist leaders, in high-necked jackets, full trousers, and boots. We chose a blue-green material that seemed a suitable dragon-colour and through make-up and hair colour tried to show that, though the dragon could take human form, he was not human. Several versions of the make-up were attempted and it is best to practise this well in advance. We finally settled for a normal skin base, and used a lot of blue and green in lines and shading, but we were not entirely satisfied. Valette coloured hair lacquer is obtainable from hairdressers' suppliers, is very effective, and brushes or washes out afterwards. The military dragon had red hair; the crafty second dragon had black hair; and we used metallic silver for the third dragon.

The costumes for this play allow infinite possibilities of style, period, nationality and mood, even within one production. The play could be presented in modern dress, either stylized or realistic, which would enhance the political aspect. But children usually prefer to dress very differently in a play. We used a mixture of styles and periods giving an over-all effect of a colourful Russian fairy tale. Although the girls in the crowd wore long skirts some of the boys wore modern clothes that were not out of place. In pantomime anything goes! There were over fifty in the cast and the total cost of materials and hire of costumes was well under twenty pounds.

It is usually impossible to make a school hall feel like a theatre. In designing a set for a play the only way is to design it for the hall, making use of any distinctive features it has. This helps to establish a feeling of locality for the actors during rehearsals, and later for the audience. From the beginning of this play we tried to create the feeling that both actors and audience were contained within an isolated town, walled in, and out of contact with the outside world.

We used the corridor on the side of the hall, and the

prompt apron steps to represent the way into the town, and fixed a canvas-painted wall to the pillars, low enough for the audience to be able to see Lancelot, and later the weavers entering the town. (This wall also served to conceal the Donkey before his appearance and also part of the equipment used for the battle sound effects.) Most of the school helped to paint sky and distant houses outside the town, which were pinned against the corridor wall and lit below by light bulbs mounted in wooden planks.

The school stage is large, and there is a small apron stage in front of the proscenium, with steps on either side. The acoustics are very bad, so we hired a scaffolding stage for fifteen pounds and placed it in front of the apron, slightly lower to provide a more interesting level. Rostra and steps were used at the back of the stage for the same purpose.

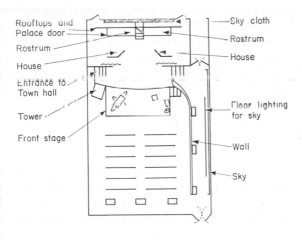

The set was kept very simple with a minimum of scene changing. The tower, stage right of the front stage, was built round two sides of some tall scaffolding used in schools for maintenance, and belonging to the Education Department. The entrance to the Town Hall was behind the tower, down the O.P. apron steps. Across the back of the stage were Gothic-shaped flats like the rooftops of a fairy-tale town, with the doorway to the Dragon's palace in the centre. Midstage behind the apron were two pairs of flats joined and painted to represent houses. For Acts One and Two the tower, the wall, and the flats were painted to represent stonework. For Act Three all the flats and the doorway at the back were reversed to provide the interior of the Palace, and were painted in brilliant colours in contrast to the earlier acts. The tower and the wall were permanent fixtures throughout the performance.

The whole of the kitchen scene in Act One was set on the front stage, and acted with the proscenium curtains closed. Entrances were made via the apron steps or through the closed curtains. Only a short interval is needed between Acts One and Two while the furniture is struck and the well for Act Two is set on the front stage. The main scenery for Act Two can be fixed securely before the performance. Having the main interval between Acts Two and Three gives time for the elaborate scene change from the town hall square to the burgomaster's palace.

The most elaborate props are the three dragons' heads, which have to look good, yet are seen so briefly. The heads were made out of chicken wire, newspaper, and glue, with some wood to support the very long necks.

At the end of Act Two, one head had to be worn by one of the dragons. The other two manipulated the heads on their arms from offstage.

Music and lighting are particularly important to this play, and must be integral parts of the production.

At first, the sound effects team had hoped to tape-record all the music and effects in one sequence, but cueing was at times so difficult that most of the effects were live and only the music was recorded. The sound effects equipment included a tape-recorder and microphone, two sheets of metal, a zinc bath, a hammer, a sword, a cymbal, a xylophone, a set of drums, and a football rattle. It is best to experiment with whatever is available. Similarly we looked for suitable music amongst the records we had in school to establish the mood of a scene, or to introduce individual characters. We created a new opening to the play using part of *The Perfect Fool* by Holst, leading up to an arresting climax on the cymbal when the crowd see Lancelot.

The play opened with the sentry standing on duty on his tower, and then the crowd moving about the town hall square buying, selling, meeting, to create the atmosphere of the evening before the public holiday when Elsa is to be sacrificed to the dragon. Lancelot's entrance along the corridor outside the city wall arrests everyone's attention, as we later learn that no stranger has entered the city for a hundred years. The crowd's reaction of fear and dislike towards the stranger can establish the situation and the relationship between the townsfolk and the hero before Act One begins. As Lancelot comes forward into the cottage the proscenium curtains close behind him to cut off the market square.

This particular crowd scene was fairly easy to produce. The townsfolk knew where they were (the town hall square), the time (the evening before the festival), and the situation (the arrival of the first stranger for a hundred years). Most of the cast had had some experience of improvisation in class. In small groups they arranged their own individual characters and relationships, and then decided what they would be doing before Lancelot arrived and how they would react to him. In this way the movement and grouping was natural and relaxed, and very little production was needed to improve its appearance. This opening scene had the advantage of giving the crowd something to do instead of waiting offstage until Act Two.

We used part of the *Capriol Suite* by Warlock for the entrance of Elsa in Act One, and the march from *The Love of Three Oranges* by Prokofiev for the entrance of the military dragon through the proscenium curtains. The noise of his arrival was provided by three small boys armed with metal sheets and a football rattle behind the closed curtains. Music was used during the blackout and changeover from the first to the second dragon. We cut the special effect of lighting Lancelot's pipe. The Burgomaster was given a traditional comedian's introduction on the xylophone, drums, and cymbal. The dragon's roars were made through the microphone and loudspeaker of the tape-recorder, as were the off-beat mocking trumpets. At times the sound effects provided a commentary on the action, for example, when the servants run to get water for the Burgomaster, and again when they make a procession with the ridiculous weapons for Lancelot. Henry spends much of Act Two running in and out for the third dragon. The xylophone accompanied him up and down the scale.

The entrance of the weavers and the donkey with the magic carpet set a problem: how to create the atmosphere of magic and hope, but also how to get the audience to react to the pantomime donkey. Flying carpets are usually associated with the Arabian Nights Entertainment, and therefore this group were dressed accordingly. It also seemed feasible that Lancelot's assistance should come from outside the town. The weavers' conversation with Henry took place while they were at the back of the hall so that the audience became aware of them. We used the Merchant's music from *The Perfect Fool* while the procession moved slowly along the corridor to the stage, and the donkey, previously hidden by the wall, achieved the surprised laugh when it came on stage.

The disappearance of Lancelot was made to an electronic sound effect while the curtains closed leaving the cat and the donkey on the stage apron.

The most alarming technical problem in the play is the battle scene in Act Two. Somehow the audience (and the actors) must be convinced that there is an overhead battle taking place between a three-headed dragon and a man on a flying carpet, during which the dragon's heads fall to the ground – and then speak. In the professional theatre they can fly scenery, project pictures, and use loudspeaker systems. Our only way was to create the effect of the scene by using crowd reaction, sound, and light. It was essential that the cast on stage, and the lighting and sounds effects teams understood exactly where the battle was meant to be taking place overhead and what was going on at any moment during this scene. The equipment for producing battle noise was divided for stereophonic effect. The metal sheets were in the corridor behind the canvas wall. The drums were on the other side of the hall.

We played three moving F.O.H. lights on the ceiling throughout the scene to represent the three heads of the dragon, and found the intermingling of red, green and purple very effective on a blue and white ceiling. We made the battle take place in one part of the sky by keeping these lights to one side of the ceiling near the noise from the metal sheets in the corridor. The crowd watched the lights on that side. At one point during the battle the dragon swooped down over the crowd and into another part of the sky. The lights swept over the crowd on the front stage, and up on the O.P. side of the ceiling, while the sound travelled by being taken up on the drums and faded out on the metal sheets. The crowd rushed from one side of the stage to the other to watch the new outbreak of battle. The conversations in the crowd had to take place during lulls in the battle when there was no noise, and the lighting was relatively normal. When the battle was at its height only the coloured lights were used. The cueing of sound and light was repetitive and became easy with practice.

As each head fell so one light moved from the ceiling down on to the stage and went out at the place where the dragon's head was to appear. This was accompanied by a dramatic roll on the drums. The crowd was used to mask the appearance of the dragon's head on the ground. They shrank together as the beam of light began to fall and broke away 'in alarm' so that the audience could see the head on the ground. We used the red light for the first dragon, the green for the second, and the purple for the third, which seemed to suit their characters.

The movement of dimmers and angling of lights can be done quite slowly and smoothly. Lancelot's speech at the end of Act Two was spoken to music and we found the theme music from the film of *The Spy who came in from the Cold* evocative. We used this music again in Act Three while Elsa described the disappearance of Lancelot. Russian folk music was used to build up the entrance of the guests to the wedding, and also to conclude the play.

In plotting the general lighting for the play we found it best to decide first how we were going to achieve the special effects, and then work out the rest of the lighting afterwards. We were able to hire inexpensively additional lights and a junior Strand Electric portable lighting bed from the Youth Office.

The important lighting effects are:

ACT I

1. The entrance of Lancelot: the problem is to light the school stage and the apron, but not the front stage where the kitchen scene is already set with the cat on stage.
2. The entrance of the first dragon: flickering lights and a cold F.O.H. spot on his entrance.
3. The blackout for the changeover from first to second dragon.

ACT 2

1. The entrance of the third dragon: We used the same F.O.H. spot as for the first dragon in Act One.
2. The entrance of the weavers.
3. The first appearance of the dragon's heads: we used

red skycloth lighting, a spot on the front batten focused on the door, and some smoke.

4. The battle.

5. Lancelot's farewell speech: after the bright lighting of the Burgomaster's scenes, eerie lighting for the dragon, and the colour of the battle, cold moonlight is effective.

ACT 3

1. The reappearance of Lancelot.

To give some idea of the amount of lighting necessary, we used eleven F.O.H. lights; three floods and a spot on the front batten; and two ground floods and an overhead strip batten to light the backcloth. We had two spots on the centre batten to give directional lighting and moonlight, and some ordinary light bulbs mounted in wood which were used to light the corridor sky. We would have used fewer lights if we had had to; we would have liked more if we could have had them.

GILLIAN PHILLIPS